SPIRIT
SHOWS
THE WAY

SPIRIT
SHOWS
THE WAY

An Ordinary Woman Blessed
with the Most Extraordinary Gift

PAM BRITTAN

Pam Brittan © 2018

All rights reserved in accordance with the
Copyright, Designs and Patents Act, 1988.

A record of this publication is available from the British Library.

ISBN: 978-1-910027-28-8

Typesetting by Wordzworth Ltd
www.wordzworth.com

Cover design by Titanium Design Ltd
www.titaniumdesign.co.uk

Printed by Lightning Source UK
www.lightningsource.com

Published by Local Legend
www.local-legend.co.uk

This book is dedicated to my wonderful family, my sisters Julie and Sandra, my daughters Michelle, Sarah and Sally, and to Don and Kate. Thank you all for your constant support.

My work is offered to all those who are going through adversity: just believe and you will realise that help is there for the asking.

And to all fledging mediums, may this book inspire you, help you to know the joy of your gift and that with it you can help many people.

Acknowledgements

I am grateful to my dear friend, Joan Harwood, who gave me the motivation to press on with my writing and helped me to get it into shape by patiently proof-reading and editing.

I thank Sue and John Thompson, and Linzi, who have believed in my ability and helped with my progress, and Anne Taylor who was my mentor as I started on my journey of serving Spirit.

Alan Cox, a friend of many years, has supported me by inviting me onto his American radio show several times. And thank you, Alison Wynne-Ryder, for encouraging me towards publication.

www.local-legend.co.uk

About the Author

Pam Brittan has been a clairvoyant medium for over thirty years and is well known throughout the UK for her wealth of spiritual knowledge and down-to-earth teaching style. She describes herself as "an ordinary woman blessed with an extraordinary gift". Pam has tirelessly shared this gift – despite many personal difficulties – through one-to-one readings and workshops, and by serving Spiritualist churches, bringing comfort and understanding to a great number of people along the way. She has created a spiritual development college course whilst also featuring on several radio shows related to the paranormal.

Her purpose in writing this book is to inspire people to realise that we can all develop our own innate psychic abilities. Even though life throws many challenges our way, a trust in Spirit will always guide us on the right path. Pam is the very embodiment of this philosophy.

She is married with four daughters, and lives in Worcestershire, UK.

Her website is *www.spiritenergyuk.co.uk*.

Previous publications

Pam has produced an online course entitled 'Empower the Hidden You'.

It is available through *www.udemy.com*.

CONTENTS

COMING HOME

Val and I sat right at the back of the room, having a giggle just like errant schoolgirls. She had finally persuaded me to accompany her to the local Spiritualist meeting, and we thought it highly amusing that the event was in a room at the British Legion Club. We had decided to go for a drink afterwards, so we'd said we would get a few spirits here then go up to the pub to have one or two there as well!

Val was desperate to hear from her mother who had died recently from leukemia, but I was apprehensive. I had an uncle who was a medium, but my family had always just accepted what he did without question; they didn't ask what it was all about and it was never referred to or discussed. To be honest, we just thought of him as 'the funny uncle' and that was as far as my knowledge went about Spiritualism.

Looking around, the congregation seemed to come from a broad spectrum of society; I don't know what I was expecting, but they all looked pretty normal people to Val and me. There was a friendly welcome for us and as we entered we were each given a hymn book. We chose our seats and the service began with a silence, a prayer and a hymn, then a talk by the medium that I found extremely thought-provoking.

The clairvoyance began after a second hymn. The medium had spoken to a couple of people and I was fascinated by what he was saying because the messages all seemed to be accepted and understood. Indeed, one of the women had broken down in tears and explained that the person who had come through was her husband; he'd been killed in a road accident at just forty-two years old. She was so thrilled but also emotional to hear from him.

I was in awe and it suddenly dawned on me that I had 'come home'. I knew now that I wasn't abnormal in 'seeing' the things I could or having the psychic feelings I did about certain events that were happening.

Suddenly, the medium came to me... In a stupor, I sensed an energy filling me, but he broke into my thoughts saying, "Are you aware that you have been called to work with Spirit?" I looked at Val and shook my head.

"No way," I whispered. The medium repeated his words and I replied, "No, I don't have any knowledge of that."

He paused and told me that he had my Uncle George here and he gave me some information that no-one else knew, not even Val who was a very close friend. It was all about the time when I was a very little girl. Uncle George had made a rocking horse for me and I had tried to feed it with sweets, which got stuck in its mouth; in the morning when I awoke, ants were climbing up towards the mouth to feed on the sugar!

"I have your attention now, good," said the medium. "It is Uncle George that is preparing the way for you to work, and it's no coincidence that you have come here tonight. You will stand on the rostrum and be known for what you do – and the work begins today."

"There's no way I would ... could do anything like that," I said.

"You have been chosen," he replied, "and although there are difficulties in your material life, all that will change. They are preparing the way." Upon that, he bestowed healing and blessing on me to help me.

Those who know me now would never believe that at that time I had no self-confidence and I would certainly not have put myself forward for spiritual work. I was in my late thirties with a young family; on top of that I was running a newsagent's with my then husband, which was a seven-day-week job with long hours. So to say I was amazed at what I'd heard would be an understatement.

The medium had also said that I had been told all this before but hadn't believed it. Then I recalled my 'funny uncle' Sid once saying, when I had not long given birth to my second daughter, that when he left off I would begin. I had dismissed this saying, "Uncle Sid, my spirits are in bottles," and laughed at the thought.

Val and I went back to the Spiritualist church time and time again. We would volunteer to make the tea and help in various other ways, following the church to many different locations within the town until they were finally able to buy their own building. During this time, I became interested in joining a development circle at the church, which was the beginning of a marvellous chapter in my life. From an early age, I had always been aware of strange happenings, seeing and feeling things as a child. But when I spoke about them to the adults in my life they were quick to dismiss these things as fantasy and even slapped me for telling lies. I learned even at that young age that this was never to be spoken of or there would be consequences...

The years of preparation

I had been placed in a children's home by my mother from the age of three and was there until I was nine. But in days gone by these places were not proper 'homes', they were more like institutions, and during those formative years I began to fear adults and never to trust promises made by anyone. So when my mother married my stepfather and finally acknowledged my presence, I was elated to be coming back to a family home at last. Yet the early experiences had taken their toll on me and it took me a while as a child just to accept that I could finally be at peace. The trouble was, although it was never threatened, I was always afraid that if I was naughty I would be sent right back to the children's home again. In a way, that subconscious thought stayed with me even into adult life.

My stepfather would never make me a promise that he could not keep and, although he was thrown in at the deep end with a nine-year old girl, he did his best to make things right. He became the Dad I'd never had. (Later, I would realise that this was my destiny – I had asked Spirit for help and here it was.) My Dad adopted me because he wanted me to have the same surname as himself and my siblings, which would mean there would not be any awkward questions from others as I was growing up.

I had two younger half-sisters whom I adored, but as I grew into a teenager my Dad and I had many differences of opinion. I became the unpaid babysitter of my younger siblings and it was expected that I would perform this duty even when I was going out with someone, working and wanting a life of my own. The upshot of this was that my Dad threw me out of home at seventeen. (Thankfully, in later life our differences were ironed out.)

So another chapter began, learning some tough life lessons.

My boyfriend's mum allowed me to stay at her house for a short time until I could find myself a place to stay. This I did, a small bedsit in the attic of a big house, sharing a bathroom with five others on the landing. Everything was on a coin meter, even the hot water for the bath, and I worked at two jobs to sustain myself. Still, I was madly in love with my boyfriend who, against all the rules, stayed overnight on a regular basis. We planned a wedding for the October of 1970, having decided to move in together because in those days married people had the best chance of getting rented accommodation. It was going to be a very low-key affair, keeping the celebrations strictly with our friends as I still had no contact with my family at the time. But events brought the marriage forward as a result of me getting pregnant!

Life really can take twists and turns unexpectedly, and the next few years proved to be a hard slog as far as I was concerned.

Not long after we had married and moved in together, my husband became unemployed, which meant that I had to go back out to work six weeks after my lovely daughter was born. Then eventually we had the opportunity to work for a newsagent's chain, which came with accommodation and wages – as well as early mornings and late nights. Trying to juggle parenthood with running a busy shop was hard work. My husband began drinking at the local public house and would often be there late into the night, which became a regular feature of my life.

After about eighteen months we moved to a bigger newsagent's shop with better accommodation and I became pregnant with my second child, another daughter. But during the birth I haemorrhaged and, added to that trauma, no-one could get in touch with my husband to tell him. Indeed, I didn't see him for two days. When he finally came into the hospital he arrived, not with presents or flowers, but with all the paperwork from the shop for me to do! Foolishly, I just got on with it.

This is what you do. Even when you feel at your lowest ebb, you brush yourself off and get on with life. Already, it was the only thing I knew how to do.

Where we lived, in a flat across the road from the shop we ran, I would have to descend three flights of stairs to be able to go out anywhere. This was difficult with a young child and a baby in the pram. Although the flat was modern and had all the facilities family life needs, it became almost a prison to me. My younger sister would come over to babysit my children each weekend so that I could carry on doing the paperwork and run the shop when my husband was 'absent'. Often, I would have to call him to say goodnight to our girls, because as usual he would go straight to the pub after closing the shop.

This was a tough time for me, because not only was I dealing with a small baby with colic, I had a young child of two and a half wanting to play outside. The flat was above some shops and although there was an area at the back it was impossible to let a child play there without supervision because there was a forty-foot drop with a small slatted wooden fence, which a small child could easily have fallen through. These circumstances now made it clear that we needed to move again. By chance, the newsagent's chain had bought another shop in a little village. The accommodation had three bedrooms, a lovely garden and good schools locally. It seemed like a dream place to move to!

Another move, another baby, and I now had three beautiful girls. During the pregnancy I suffered a thrombosis clot in my leg which was supposed to mean I had to rest as much as I could… but my husband's promotion to Area Manager gave him the excuse once again to stay out until very late. As soon as the baby was born I was sterilised, on advice from my consultant because of my medical history; yet when I returned home after having my third child and an operation, I was given the keys by my husband to open the shop the next morning. Foolishly, I fell into line and did what was asked!

The consequences of this foolishness in returning to work was that the blood clot went to my lung and I was confined to hospital for three months. My husband's sister volunteered to look after the children at this time and I was so grateful to her. I'd had a lucky escape – one of my lives had certainly been used up.

Following this ordeal, life returned more or less to normal and I was reasonably content for a little while. I had made friends with the locals and a lady who had recently come to live in one of the terraced houses across the road became a close friend. Her name was Val. Indeed, her son had been born twelve months before my youngest daughter, and because I was so busy in the shop she would look after my baby and take her shopping in the pram, with her son in a seat on the top. Bless her, she kept me sane!

It had been a very traumatic time. Looking back, this was a time when I had started to believe that there was 'something more' out there. Each night I would pray to a higher power, wanting some help, and each day would be convinced that something would happen…

Out of the blue

Still, my life continued to be challenging. My husband lived his life as if he were single, staying out night after night and coming home worse for wear with drink. Our work was also our home, so it was important to me to keep some normality within our family for the sake of the children. I would simply dust myself down and get on with it all. What else could I do? There was the daily drama of raising three girls then aged between five and nine, and a busy newsagent's to run from 6 a.m. until 6 p.m. singlehandedly.

It was difficult to get things organised so that I could get out and have some time for myself, but I wanted to keep the momentum going by attending the church regularly. With the help of the girls who used to work for me on a Saturday as babysitters, it was a godsend for me to be able to have any time away even if it was only for a short period.

Val and I attended the church whenever we were able to, even becoming members, which meant that we were able to 'sit in circle'. At first, I didn't have a clue what that meant, but one week we were invited to attend on the Thursday evening. Val was very apprehensive about it all, but somehow I took it all in my stride. Little did I know then that this would be the start of things to come for me. The lady who ran the circle, Anne Taylor, was to become my mentor and teacher, responsible for me beginning to work for Spirit. At this development circle there would be a meditation to take us deeper and deeper into a different level of consciousness, so that we could tune into either our higher selves or to the spirit world. (The reason it is called a circle is because all the people sit together in a circle.)

During these times I had some wonderful experiences. Once during the meditation I was taken on a boat into 'the Crystal Caves' and told to choose a crystal. I asked whether the colour mattered and was told just to choose; we would be told what it meant afterwards. At the time I just chose a clear quartz and knew it was significant for something. When we came out of the meditation, Anne told me it was very important as the clear quartz can clarify 'spiritual seeing'. I was troubled by this, but also curious. Another time I found myself being taken up a hill by a Native American Indian brave; his hair was tied back and he had one feather hanging from it, which he kept pointing to as if it were important. After the meditation there wasn't time to talk to Anne about it, so I jotted it down for a later date. However, this was going to become very significant.

It was difficult to meditate at home and sometimes I would get this feeling that I was being 'watched' and couldn't understand why...

Then one day Val invited me over to have a cuppa with her at lunchtime. In those days, the shop was usually closed for an hour each day so it was during one of these long lunch breaks that we were able to take advantage and have a natter. Val had told me earlier that she would leave the front door on the latch so I could walk straight in and not ring the doorbell. Her place was an old-fashioned terrace house where you walked straight into the front room from the front door; a door opposite led to another room where the stairs were accessed by a door in the left-hand corner. The kitchen was long and narrow, at the back of the house; the back door led to a small courtyard which then opened onto a tiny back garden. As I went into the house through the front door straight into the living room, I saw a lady sitting in a chair; she had dark hair, wore glasses, and was dressed in a dark coat and flowered skirt.

"Hello," I said, "I've come for a cuppa with Val."

I knew that Val was in the kitchen because she had called out that she was putting the kettle on, so I walked towards the other door and called to her, "Oh, so sorry Val, I didn't realise you had visitors." Val came in immediately and I was astonished to find that the lady had disappeared. When I described her, Val told me it had been her mother! I had never met Val's Mum and had never seen a picture of her.

"Well, she says she's alright and you are to stop worrying now," I said.

"How do you know that?" Val replied. She looked at me gob-smacked, shaking her head and sitting down with a bump, wiping her tears because she had been silently saying to her Mum, "Why won't you come to me? All I ask is for you to tell me that you're alright." Well, I was so taken aback – I really did not expect that to happen, and it came right out of the blue.

"We definitely need that cuppa now!" I said.

We sat silently drinking our tea for a few moments until Val said, "You have to get on with this now." She hesitated and then said, "Maybe I was sent to show you and take you to the church. I have a feeling that nothing will get in the way now, not for you or for me."

We continued sipping our tea, deep in thought. Val had told me earlier that her marriage was in jeopardy and in an effort to save it they had decided to move up to Berwick, where her husband's sister lived. I was devastated. Val was now a close friend, we told each other everything and I felt that if she left it would be quite a while before she returned, if at all. Telephone calls would just not be the same and I was dreading the day she would leave. The news made me so unhappy, because it was only Val and the church keeping me believing that somehow things would change for the better.

The day she left, I cried myself to sleep. But the next morning at 5.30 a.m. I dusted myself off and opened the shop, ready for the next episode of my life. If I was chosen to work with Spirit, when was that to happen – and how?

SIGNPOSTS

Over the next eighteen months several significant things happened. My husband's mother died from a stroke. Her death was no surprise as she had been comatose for several weeks, so it was a blessed release really. However, it still had an impact on our lives. Then my husband lost his driving licence for a year because he was over the alcohol limit; if he wanted to continue being Area Manager he was told that he would have to pay a driver out of his salary. We certainly didn't live richly. The house came with the job, we were paid on a commission basis from the shop takings and this commission had also to provide money for staff wages. This situation meant we were very much in the hands of market forces as the less the shop took the tighter our end salary became. There had been many redundancies at the big local employers at that time and these had an obvious knock-on effect. Working a twelve-hour shift, keeping the household going and trying to be a good Mum all took its toll, but stoically I just got on with it, hopefully hiding my weariness from everyone.

I revelled in the evenings out at the church, sitting in the power of Spirit and receiving some wonderful information. Time and time again I was told from the rostrum not to give up and that I was now 'on the pathway to serve Spirit' – the difference now was that I had begun to believe this could really be possible. Bromsgrove Church became my spiritual haven. It was the only place I felt I was at home. My actual home life had become so stressful and I felt completely isolated, trying to juggle everything without the support of someone by my side to help me. The person who should have been by my side was so busy keeping the public house in funds he had lost sight of the fact that he was a father and husband.

Every year a trip was arranged by the church to go to the Arthur Findlay College in Stansted for a week, called the Physical Phenomena Week. The building that had become the college was left to the Spiritualist movement by Sir Arthur Findlay, for the development and training of mediums and healers. The members who wanted to go on this trip all saved a little each week towards it and, as the time got nearer, I was apprehensive but determined to go. I had to make sure that all would be well at home, the children well cared-for and the shop in order, before I could go off for a week. My husband was not a man I could rely on to help me, but at least he did arrange a suitable temporary replacement for the running of the shop while I was gone.

Prior to taking this journey, I also had the wonderful news (for me) that Val was returning and would be there when I came back. I was overjoyed as I had missed her so much.

A few days before the trip, I dreamed that the Native American Indian brave came to me again. He showed me a semicircle of mountains and pointed once again to the single feather tied to his hair at the side of his head. He told me, "All this can be yours. You must strive towards it." I awoke knowing this was significant and wrote it down in a little exercise book next to my bed. I had been told to write stuff down because sometimes we may not understand it all at first but we would later.

Another dream I had was quite significant and the memory stayed with me throughout my spiritual development. In this dream I was taken to attend a special meeting where my Uncle Sid and Auntie Elsie (both in the Spiritualist movement at the time) beckoned me towards a huge table and sat me down. The room seemed enormous and echoed with voices and musical sounds. As I watched, a huge book was opened before me on the table and Uncle Sid told me to sign; I was signing an important contract, he said. Somehow, I felt it was right and didn't question what I was being told. Behind a desk was a man dressed all in white, with white hair and a long white beard. His eyes met mine as I put my signature in this book and he smiled. No words were exchanged. When I awoke, I recorded this dream in the little bedside book too.

At the time, I thought little of this 'signpost' but that is exactly what it was. My Uncle Sid later told me that I had been shown I was signing up to serve Spirit. The man behind the desk has since revealed himself to me as a great philosopher guide who has worked with me for some time now. (I laugh to myself these days because when I'd awoken from that dream it was so intense, I thought I had been in the presence of God; it was in fact this very evolved spirit guide called Abraham.) Uncle Sid smiled knowingly and nodded as he said, "This is a sure sign that you are now on the right pathway."

I was now beginning to understand the work that both my auntie and uncle did and was in awe of their knowledge. They had travelled the length and breadth of the country by public transport to serve the Spiritualist churches; indeed, they ran a church themselves for some time. They were very dedicated and I hope that the work I have been doing makes them proud, because it is humbling to me that I was chosen to continue their work.

My first trip to the Arthur Findlay College was so awe-inspiring. I met several people of like mind and realised that I was not unique, there are lots of people who can see and hear and who aspire to work with and serve Spirit. I was put into the group for new learners and very quickly settled into the routine of this place. The tutorials began after breakfast and went on until 9.30 p.m. It was an amazing experience.

The first day, we met our tutor and he arranged us in a circle. There were about eighteen of us newbies of different ages, backgrounds, even from different countries, but the one common factor was that we were all yearning for some spiritual knowledge. We were told to sit and follow his words in a meditation, into a Native American Indian campsite where we sat in a circle with the elder tribesmen and took note of what was said and done. I followed the instructions and was amazed to feel the energy of this circle very intensely, even more so than during our meetings at the church. Perhaps it was the place being continuously used for spiritual enlightenment that explained the strength of the energy.

Then I saw my Indian brave there, again pointing to his feather and telling me that the answer would come now. He showed me a pathway covered in brambles and told me that at the moment we couldn't pass through, but in the future the pathway would be open when I was cleared. Although I questioned this to myself at the time, I later realised that he simply meant the time was not quite ready.

When we were told to come back to normal consciousness, I mentally made a note of all that I'd been shown; but because I didn't want people to think I was completely mad, I didn't relate all that had happened to the group. However, during this session one of the German ladies present asked the tutor what all the feathers in the headdress of the Indian braves meant. His first words astonished me: he said that having one feather in the hair meant 'a communicator who comes in peace'. To me this was really significant because 'my' Indian brave had pointed this out so many times to me. I now knew that he must

14

be my guide. I have to say at this point that I knew I was receiving information – but not how, from where or from whom. So to realise that I had a guide was an eye-opener for me.

That evening there was a demonstration of trance mediumship in one of the rooms, open to all the groups. Watching this medium at work was fascinating, seeing the changes on their face and even feeling the changing atmosphere in the room made me thirsty to know more about this 'physical phenomenon'.

During the week's stay we saw many demonstrations, some of clairvoyance, some of trance and some of other kinds of physical mediumship. The one that stands out by far to me was when all the groups were herded into 'The Red Room', which was a room in the basement of the building that had the walls painted red. In the corner was a three-sided box, called a 'cabinet', for the medium to sit in. (For those readers who have never seen this, a cabinet is often used for physical trance mediumship. It usually has a red light placed on the top so that the audience can see the phenomena being emitted; normal light can be dangerous for the medium. The cabinet is an instrument that enables spiritual energy to build up within its space, helping the medium to connect with Spirit.) Well, from my earliest days I have been afraid of the dark and enclosed spaces...

"If you are afraid of being closed in or of the dark," someone announced, "you must leave now." Anne was seated next to me and she reassured me by squeezing my hand. So I stayed put – but was terrified!

The lights went out and the room was completely blacked out except for the small red light above the cabinet. I couldn't even see my friends either side of me. After a few moments the medium, who was a man, began talking in a female voice and called out to "someone behind the contraption". In the interests of science, investigators were taking photographs of the medium during the demonstration and their camera was the contraption he was referring to. The answer came and the evidence of Spirit was outstanding. The voice was recognised by a lady as being her mother's and she was overwhelmed, not only with the message but also by the way in which it came.

As the demonstration proceeded I noticed lights coming from the box, overhead and onto the ceiling, and I kept blinking to make sure that what I was seeing was real. I was astounded, but until we came out and discussed it all I didn't mention the lights; I thought, as we always do at first, that it was just my imagination. In the discussions it transpired that many others had seen the lights too, another confirmation for me. Unfortunately, Health and Safety rules mean that The Red Room does not exist now, although there are many other ways of seeing these phenomena at the Arthur Findlay College.

This was a week that would stay with me forever and even now I am elated to relate this to you because these things are what proved to me beyond doubt that there is more to life than we know. During this time, we were also able to book private readings for ourselves, so I took the opportunity and went along at the allotted time. I was told some very personal things, in particular that everything would change soon: at first I would think that events were devastating but they would prove to bring a change for the better in the end.

"In the meantime, Spirit will show you many things and take you to many places," the medium told me. Again, this proved to me beyond doubt that communication with the spirit world can and does happen.

I didn't want that week to end. For the first time in my life, I felt I had found the niche that was meant for me. I knew when I arrived back to my normal life at home that things would have to change. But how and when? I could only see 'more of the same' and in those days my self-esteem was very low; I didn't have the courage to take the next steps on my own.

But it was all planned out. Destiny has a way of getting us to the right place at the right time.

DOORS OPEN

I t took a while to get my feet firmly back on the ground after that week of being completely immersed in spiritual things. But back to normal was the name of the game, doing the twelve-hour stint at work and meeting the normal motherly demands of small children.

Val and I had a reunion with tears and hugs. It was lovely to see her back within reach and we settled into a routine of seeing each other whenever we could and attending the church together. She didn't want to come and sit in the development circle with me, but encouraged me to keep going because she could see how much it had meant to me.

There was a need to expand the shop area and it was thought that this could be done by knocking down the wall that went into the kitchen of the living quarters. A friend of my husband, who was a building contractor, gained the contract to do the work but what was meant to be a six-week job ended up taking six months. It was a nightmare and meant that I couldn't get to church as often as I would like. Also, my youngest daughter suffered from whooping cough and was very poorly, all the dust and the dirt seeming to make her worse. Again, this was another thing my husband didn't even acknowledge at the time.

Then, building the kitchen extension revealed that the staircase was crumbling from underneath (the building was two hundred-year old cottages joined together) so it turned out that a lot of unexpected work needed to be done on the premises. Now here I was, still trying to keep the shop running, looking after a very poorly little girl and two other children, and on top of that having to climb a ladder to go to bed at night!

During this time my youngest daughter kept telling me that she could see a lady in the house wearing Victorian clothes; I must admit that I had felt this energy as well but was just too busy to tune into it. However, as time went by, and even after the renovations had all been completed, my daughter would never climb the stairs to go to the toilet on her own without me being at the bottom calling her name. My own childhood experiences had taught me that I must not frighten my daughter, nor ignore what she was saying, so I just told her this was nothing to worry about and the lady was looking after us.

Yet I was not at all sure about this and felt uneasy, because during the renovations this lady became more noticeable and would come to me almost nightly while I was in bed. One night, she stood at the bottom of the bed and I could clearly see her, so I sat up and just calmly asked her what she wanted. She told me that my time here in this place was coming to an end and that she would be glad to have some peace and quiet again! She seemed very cross but I didn't fear her; I thanked her for coming and asked her not to frighten my daughter anymore. Again, my little notebook came out and I jotted her words in it, not realising how significant those words would be in the coming year.

It seemed that, the very few times I could attend a church service during all of this, the messages were constantly reassuring me that 'the time was near' when working for Spirit would become important to me. As you can tell by what was going on in my life, I wondered how this could possibly happen. It just didn't seem likely. Nothing was changing as such and no wonder I was stressed. How could I accept the burden of more work?

At long last the work in the shop was over and life began to get back to some sort of normality. My husband was back driving again but hadn't learned his lesson. I usually didn't see him until the pubs turned out so the everyday running of things was still left for me to sort out. Then one night he just didn't come home. I was worried sick and called the local pub where he often drank, only to be told that he'd left around 11.30 p.m. the night before. I called a friend of his, who promised he would try to find him and see me later, but I heard nothing more. Then at 10.30 the next morning he simply walked in through the shop and went straight upstairs. After serving a customer, I followed him and ran up the stairs to confront him.

He had been arrested and held overnight for drink driving again. This meant he was no longer able to hold down the job of Area Manager and would have to come back into the shop. Somehow, inside me I knew that this was the beginning of the end.

Knowing this and realising it are two different things. We try to ignore our inner voices and carry on regardless. My husband always had plausible reasons for why we should be doing this or that and, the weak person I was then, I listened and thought he must know best. But it was now getting financially more difficult to pay the staff, which meant I had to be in the shop for a lot longer than normal. Moreover, doing anything like going to church that required me to pay for babysitters was now out of the question.

Many further events occurred in the next two years that eventually led to my husband being called in to the Head Office. I was not allowed to be privy to the conversation, but it transpired that we would now have to leave the shop and our home of twelve years. We had worked for this company for seventeen years with hardly any trouble at all.

This was the turning of another corner. I had been asking Spirit for some help to stop the unhappiness I had been feeling for a very long time – I can tell you, I was extremely tired and stressed – but of course I was worried about the outcome of this situation. My children were now nine, thirteen and sixteen and for them it was devastating. I felt numb, knowing that we just needed to find a home, and so stoically I just kept going. I have always been a cup-half-full kind of girl and looked on this as just another chapter in my life. In a way, I saw it as a T-junction in the road and we just needed to find the right way now to get on with life.

A home was found, chosen by my husband who, in his infinite wisdom, decided to use the little money we had left over to decorate and build a new fireplace in the house (which was completely unnecessary). Of course, the money ran out and the kitchen was left half-done, and we were without anything financially to keep us going for the coming weeks.

Yet a strange thing happened during this period… Our dog Penny was always by my side and there were times when she was my 'agony aunt', hearing all my troubles and woes and listening to my fears. She had only ever known the shop and the accommodation there in her life, but seemed very settled when we eventually moved. When I went back to the shop with Penny a few days after the move to collect a couple of items I had left behind, she adamantly refused to cross the threshold into the building, even to the point of really yelping when I tried to coax her. I took this as another sign that Spirit had meant all these things to happen (and that the Victorian lady didn't want us back!).

Soon after this, I was bemoaning my troubles to Val and she persuaded me to come to the church with her – the first time in a long while for me – and she would get her husband to take us and even put money for me on the offering plate. No, I didn't even have the funds to do that. In a world of my own I sat in the peace of the church, the turmoil still going on within me, wondering what was going to happen next. Then Val nudged me: the medium had picked me out, speaking about my Uncle George who was showing me the rocking horse again. I was told that although things looked now as though the end of the world was nigh, I must not despair because this was all part of a process for the next three years that would lead to a much better life for me – and to the journey of serving Spirit.

When I got home, all that was in my mind was "three years". Oh my goodness, how was I to endure all this for another three years? And as far as serving Spirit was concerned, how the devil was that going to happen? My heart was breaking. I felt in such despair, how I didn't go under is beyond me.

New skills

My eldest daughter began college to train in catering, and she had also met someone she thought was 'the one' for her. She was still young and I was hoping that she would wait a little while before wanting to settle down; but our home life was hardly a bed of roses so I couldn't blame her for wanting out.

Val was looking for a new job and persuaded me to go with her to the Job Centre. I had been searching in vain for something other than retail but because my secretarial skills were now outdated it was hard to find that niche. So, with the promise of buying me coffee, bless her, Val cajoled me into going with her. Once again she was taking me by the hand at the right time to open a door for me. A training course was being advertised at the Job Centre to get people to update their secretarial skills in order to return to work after a gap. It was Heaven-sent. It even paid transport costs and would run from the September until the December of that year. I instantly signed up for it and only wished I could have afforded to take Val for a slap-up meal in gratitude.

When I had trained initially, we had used the old-fashioned manual typewriter and if any copies were needed we used carbon paper while typing. So word processing and computers were a marvellous new concept for me. The course was great and when I left with my updated skills I was ready for the work market; indeed, I signed up with an agency immediately. Home life was still fraught with problems, but at least I could now tackle the financial aspect of it all, with a wage finally coming in. During the next twelve months I became established in a steady job, working for a firm whose parent company was in Canada. They insisted that everyone paid into a health insurance scheme in case of long-term sickness or terminal illness, and at the time I bemoaned the cost of course – well, how often do you claim on these insurances? Yet you will read later how important even this part of 'the plan' was!

My daughter became pregnant and married her boyfriend. So here was another drama to be overcome, with money to be found so that they could have a decent type of wedding. Afterwards, they had to live in our house until suitable accommodation could be found, and to say this was a difficult time is an understatement. But a mother looks after her chicks, no matter what; she was still my baby and all I wanted to do was to protect her. Then she was rushed into hospital with pre-eclampsia on Christmas Eve and her baby was born prematurely by emergency caesarean section on December 28th. Seeing this little mite weighing 3 lbs, and my daughter with wires and intravenous drips, broke my heart. And once again I was having to cope with this on my own.

I realised with increasing clarity that my marriage was making me deeply unhappy and, although I had been like the ostrich and buried my head in the sand, I had to face this head on and do something about it. But no, now was still not yet the time. As a new year dawned, my mother became quite ill with mini-strokes and my sister-in-law had also been diagnosed with cancer; within the next year they both died, my Mum in the April with a massive stroke and my sister-in-law in the December. During this year, my husband was back driving again and at long last in work but I very rarely saw him. I basically washed and ironed his clothes, provided meals, and tried to be civil when we had conversations.

I attended church as often as I could and started to go to the development circle again. This seemed to be the only bit of sanity left to me. Anne decided she would take me under her wing; she took me along to a couple of churches to work with her initially, then put my name forward to attend the 'novice scheme' at the church, for training mediums in their presentation on the rostrum. Now, no-one can give you the gift of mediumship, that is yours, but this kind of scheme enables you to stand in front of an audience and to understand how to present your messages from the spirit world as well as giving a talk to inspire and bring joy to the people. I was very reluctant to attend this course at first because of all the 'stuff' going on in my personal life, but concentrating on something else so worthwhile was a real-life saver.

Mediumship is not the easiest of pathways to take.
Often, mediums find themselves having to endure many life challenges.
But this is not a 'test', it is to strengthen our faith.

Finally, my daughter and her little family found accommodation and moved out. They were followed months later by my middle daughter, who was approaching seventeen and also wanting to be independent and move in with her boyfriend. They were still so very young and I often wonder whether these things would have happened if they'd had a proper father figure. Could I have done better by my children? Well, none of us is perfect and we try our best with the circumstances we are dealt at the time. So much was changing in a short time and the trauma of losing my parent and much-loved sister-in-law was taking its toll on me as well.

My middle daughter then gave us the news that she was pregnant. She seemed quite happy about this at the time, but when you are young you do not realise the consequences of your actions until much later. All I could do was take her in my arms and hug her. They had to live with us part-time and with her mother-in-law the remaining days until they could afford to get a home of her own, and this went on until her son was six months old. Once again, not the easiest of times. But battling through had become the name of the game for me.

Even with all this going on, I continued on my spiritual journey, attending my course and being put through the paces of a novice. This course was for twelve months and, having no transport at the time, it was difficult for me to get to certain places. Anne helped in the early days and then I got the opportunity to buy an old car from a chap at work. My sister helped with the funds so this enabled me to get mobile.

A guy at work had been coming to pick me up every day in return for petrol money; it was cheaper and easier for me than the bus, he lived locally and would be going that way in any case. Once I had my own car, we took it in turns. He became a sounding board for me and our conversations were important because he would often tell me that I was worth more than the work I was doing and the other people there. The fact that I was now confidently doing quite an important job made me realise that, yes, I was worthy and not the useless idiot I was often told I was by my husband. My self-esteem began to develop a little.

Being a 'novice' meant we were chosen to serve different churches around the country, often three of us together taking it in turns on the rostrum, giving clairvoyance, saying a prayer and doing the talk. This was nerve-racking to say the least! At first, my fears made me worry whether I was going to get a link with Spirit at all. Did I really know what I was talking about when it came to address the congregation? And saying prayers out loud was something I just couldn't seem to master initially. But confidence slowly came and I learned to trust what I was told to say by Spirit, to stop analysing it and just say it as it came.

For example, I remember that during this time I spoke to a gentleman and suddenly was given an image of the aviary that belonged to my Auntie Lil's mother-in-law, known as Granny Smith. So I knew that the man in the spirit world had kept birds, pigeons in fact, and I relayed this to the gentleman sitting in the congregation. I also knew that this man was a grandfather, because he had told me so. Then the grandfather was showing me a pigeon he was letting go into the air and watching it circle above with tears in his eyes. I felt a sadness with this but didn't understand why.

So I dithered with trying to make sense of all this until in the end I just told the gentleman what I had seen. He replied that his grandfather had kept pigeons and that they'd won prizes, but he was sad because one of his favourite birds had not come home and was never seen again. So you see, here I was trying to make sense of the information but, by simply giving the evidence as it came, it all made sense to the gentleman. That was very much another learning curve for me. The responsibility of it all still weighed heavily upon me. After all, we are dealing with messages that have come from loved ones in the spirit world, so they must be right and given with care. Eventually, after completing and passing the course, we novices were let out on our own to serve the various churches, for which bookings came in fast and furiously.

One day during meditation, I asked my Indian brave what his name was and he told me, "Crowfoot." "What a silly name," I thought, this has got to be from my own imagination; indeed, I even said as much to him and asked for physical proof before I could believe those words. Haven't I got a cheek, questioning those in the spirit world? But it was me I doubted, not them, because I'd learned that you only have to ask and they will answer. (Look for acknowledgement to come three times in different forms, then you will know that it comes from Spirit.)

Soon afterwards, while travelling to a church along the M5/M6 corridor, which is notorious for traffic jams, a van came alongside me and completely cut me up so that I had to brake suddenly. The company name on the back of the van was 'Crowfoot Carriers'! I was astonished and said out loud to myself that if ever there was physical proof then this was it; I thanked Crowfoot for this evidence and carried on with my journey. Crowfoot was the first guide made known to me, although other guides came to me later as I developed my spiritual gift.

I have learned that guides and angels are with us whether we pursue a spiritual path or not. Many people ask what the difference is between them. Well, guides have lived on this Earth and have had experience of life – they may even have lived many lifetimes – so they understand the complexities of our times as human beings. Angels are from another dimensional level, though; they have never lived on Earth and are spirit beings helping mankind in various areas of our lives. We are all blessed with a guardian angel who has the task of safeguarding us right from the beginning of our journey throughout this lifetime.

Here's another indication of how we must trust Spirit and what they are saying. It came when serving a church on my own for the very first time. I was asked to step into the medium's room and sit quietly before coming into the church. I was almost shaking with nerves, despite my travelling companion Val sitting in the church, having assured me that everything was going to be fine. In that room, I closed my eyes and did a short meditation asking for help and guidance: I was told I had to go to 'the lady in a purple coat', so now I felt ready and sure they had given me the right information.

I went onto the rostrum on my own for the first time and looked around – but there was no lady with a purple coat! I led the congregation in a prayer and then we began singing the first hymn, all the time with me scanning the audience. Just as we got to the last verse of the hymn, in walked the lady wearing a purple coat. Was I relieved! I have learned that people often let you down, but Spirit never will. Here was clear proof, because of course I had not seen a purple coat when I'd come into the church. Spirit will always guide and help you if you just listen to them.

When I visited my Uncle Sid he told me that he was very proud of me, he applauded me and told me not to worry and that 'all would come right in the end'. I had spoken to him about my personal challenges, so he knew that it was a struggle for me to continue the spiritual journey. But he was sure that somehow I would do what was needed to get there.

Was I now on my way? Little did I know there were even more challenges to be endured. I think Uncle Sid had sensed this and had really tried to reassure me because he knew there were tougher times ahead...

BELIEVE IN GUIDANCE

During this period, I had the opportunity to go to the Arthur Findlay College again, though this time with a little more experience of spiritual things. My friend Pat was coming too and I told her that she would have a marvellous experience at the college, so there were great expectations from our little group going to Stansted. Anne had said this was going to be our last visit because numbers were dropping and it had become a difficult task trying to please everyone. Although we were sad about this, we realised that things were also changing at the college. Still, the fun and laughter we'd had would always remain with us.

I had been to Stansted several times by now for Open Days and my understanding was growing, but I still felt I was in the learning stage. Indeed, even after all these years I am still learning and in awe of the spiritual happenings in my life. We should never let the ego rule, always being humbled by this gift; it is given by Spirit and they can take it away if it isn't used correctly.

Pat and I found ourselves in the same tutorial group but by midweek we were both feeling a little disheartened with the teacher. He seemed to be so full of ego and constantly talking about himself, and we found ourselves just listening to his achievements rather than him giving us the information we were sorely looking for to enhance our spiritual development. When we met for lunch as usual, Pat said that if there was something marvellous to happen then it had better hurry up and do so! I laughed at the look on her face. She was very down-to-earth and stood no nonsense, and was on the verge of telling our tutor to come down off his pedestal and begin giving us some proper input.

That afternoon, all the groups came together in one room to see a 'transfiguration' medium at work. What is transfiguration? Well, in this case the medium would go into trance and a spiritual substance called 'ectoplasm' would build up into a mask over her face to show the loved one who is in the spirit world. Not all mediums can do this, and even for those who are so gifted it takes years of dedication to get to this level. Our Bromsgrove Group sat together and were in awe of what was about to happen. The medium sat in the trance cabinet. It was October and the evenings were already drawing in early as we gathered in the afternoon; the curtains were drawn and the side lights dimmed just to show a glimmer of light for the audience to be able to see. Two experienced mediums sat either side of the cabinet; there was a seat for the medium and a chair opposite her for the recipient to sit when a message was given. The audience were seated in an arc to watch what was taking place.

The medium went into trance in the cabinet and then called out the name of someone to come forward and sit in the chair. This gentleman did as he was asked and when the medium began to speak he gasped, seeing on the medium's face a mask of his wife looking back at him. From our seats we could see this mask building up from ectoplasm into the shape of the wife's face. The message was profound too, speaking about the man's daughter and a new grandson who had recently arrived. He was so taken aback that when the message ended he stood up and moved forward to kiss the medium, but was very quickly prevented from doing so by one of the 'bodyguard' mediums at the side! Touch can be very dangerous for a transfiguration medium in trance as it can bring them suddenly into consciousness, causing the ectoplasm to rush inside them and potentially cause damage. This is why two experienced mediums sat at the side to prevent this happening.

Next, Pat's name was called. She was expecting someone else to go forward so I nudged her and whispered, "This is for you, Pat, go on, go to the chair."

She sat down and saw her Mum looking back at her. Pat had nursed her Mum for a year with a cancer condition. Also, in the past Pat had suffered several miscarriages and had a baby stillborn, so she had never had the joy of rearing her own children. Her Mum's message was so profound that all the Bromsgrove lot were in tears. Pat had waited a long time for confirmation that her Mum was okay and to hear about her babies in the spirit world. Well, this day she not only had confirmation about how her Mum was doing but the message gave Pat some news about her Dad, and even information about events she could look forward to in the future (which did come true).

We were all agog, but for me it was also confirmation of what I had been told by Spirit to tell Pat a few months previously, about this trip being important. None of us knew the itinerary of the week until we arrived, so seeing the transfiguration medium had been a complete surprise. Pat had certainly had her marvellous moment.

More was to come, for me at least. The next day we were back into our groups and talking about what had happened; this time, thankfully, a new tutor had taken over so we were both relieved. She got us sitting on chairs forming a circle. At the back of the room, on tables behind a screen, were containers of chemicals for developing photographs. The tutor told us that we were going to do 'scotography', where Spirit can cause images to appear on photographic paper directly. The paper was put on our laps, then we were to go into a meditation and see what would come out on the paper when it was developed. During this time, the tutor would also put a piece of blank photographic paper in the middle of the circle and she said that something would come out on this as a message for someone in the room.

We all looked at each other, this certainly being something we had never done before. Before the meditation began, the tutor asked us to think of something we would like to see on the paper. Then we sat quietly in the darkness, going into an altered state of consciousness. It had been a very busy week, with late nights and early mornings and we had been to all the seminars we could pack into the short time of being there. So I'm afraid that when we started to meditate my only thought was to develop a rose on the paper, then I just fell into a short sleep.

Science would say, of course, that every piece of photographic paper would remain blank when processed. However, this afternoon every piece had some image on it and some were even in colour. Mine had a rose beginning to form in the corner of the paper, but in the middle was also the skeleton of a foot. I wondered whether this could be a reference to Crowfoot... When the tutor developed the piece of paper in the middle of the circle there was the profile view of a Native American Indian. The tutor was told that this was someone's guide and he was from the Crow tribe. Looking at the foot on my paper and hearing this from the tutor, I immediately knew the information was for me: it was my guide, who was indeed of the Crow tribe.

I was amazed. Spirit always finds a way to inform us when we least expect it. As I have said before, if you receive information three times then it comes from Spirit to confirm what you have already been told. Don't dismiss anything! Keep a little book handy and write information down; it may not be applicable immediately but it will be in the future.

These were wonderful experiences that will always stay with me. Transfiguration mediums are few because of the rare gift and the sheer energy it takes for this to happen. To see the mask was an especially enriching experience and it shows us that there are many things we do not know. Equally, when genuine information comes out of the blue to confirm things, then we must believe what we hear and see. The Arthur Findlay College is still run today with many courses to enrich and develop budding mediums or just to educate those interested in spiritual phenomena. It holds regular Open Days so I would urge anyone to attend a course or go along for a day.

Back in the real world

Things were happening that would alter the course of my life again. Prior to the house move, I'd had laser treatment to clear some cancer cells that had been discovered during a routine cancer smear test. (Ladies, never think you do not need this test because, believe me, it saved my life.) For five years following this I had regular smear tests which always came back negative – until now.

On top of this, I was getting a variety of other symptoms such as numbness, my foot seemingly dragging behind me, and my balance going out of kilter. One day, my left side seemed to go completely numb. The GP was called, she told me to rest and that she would come out and see me next day. I assumed this was because of all the stress in my life; by now I literally had a job getting in and out of bed and I felt helpless. As mentioned earlier, I was fortunately in a private health scheme at work, so I was referred very quickly to specialists.

An MRI scan revealed the early stages of multiple sclerosis (MS). I carried on trying to stay positive and not worry the family too much, but I had to stay off work because it took a while to get me back to walking up and down stairs and leading a normal sort of life. In fact, I had a very bad episode at the beginning of this period, which completely incapacitated me.

At first, remember, I had grumbled about having to pay into this insurance, but now I was reaping the benefits of it and having my salary paid even though I was far too poorly to go to work. Indeed, I never did go back to that job again. My boss was extremely understanding though; he came to see me and told me that if ever I was ready to go back to work, there would always be a job for me. But because of the amount of time needed for me to recover, they had to replace me. Even after several weeks I was not fully able to get on with everyday life, so I knew that they could not keep that position open any longer.

Then the gynaecologist told me that further scans and tests had revealed the possibility of cancer again and advised me to have a full hysterectomy, which was arranged in less than six weeks.

I made up my mind now to seek a divorce. All these different events made me realise that my life might not be very long, so if I only had a short amount of time to live then I wanted a quality of life during that time and not to live as I had been doing anymore. Of course, I also realised that my husband would not support me during my illness and there was enough to deal with without any more aggravation from him.

When at last I could get out of the house into the High Street, I found myself one morning automatically walking towards a solicitor's office with the thought of making an appointment to get advice about putting separation or divorce proceedings in motion. I was still apprehensive, though. Was this the journey I really wanted to take? Indeed, when I'd married I assumed at the time it was for life; perhaps this is a very old-fashioned concept today, but it was something I didn't take lightly. The lady at Reception was putting down the telephone as I approached. I asked for an appointment and was told I was in luck, someone had just cancelled and an appointment was free the next day. Again, I'm sure this was Spirit taking action, knowing that I was hesitating and wondering whether this was the right thing to do. Even with all that had happened during the years of my marriage, it was still hard for me to break the bonds. But it had to be done.

The new pathway had now started!

My spiritual work during this time had been put on hold. I couldn't get out and about and was very much in the hands of spiritual healers who, bless them, gave me 'absent healing'. This is when someone can 'send' healing to a person in need. You don't necessarily have to be a trained healer for this to work. Yes, very often churches have healing books to enter names into for this absent healing to be given by their qualified healers. But if you know anyone in need, Spirit will send this healing to them on your behalf if you simply go into a quiet meditation, think of the person in need and visualise sending a ball of energy their way.

Now, you might have thought that all this was enough for me to deal with. But coming over the horizon there was more that no-one, not even me, could have predicted. Out of the blue one day came an envelope from the Salvation Army. I opened it up and inside there was a letter from a lady who told me that she was my half-sister on my father's side, and that I also had a full-blood brother. Nothing could have prepared me for this and I honestly thought they had the wrong person. I spoke about this to my good friend Val, and she advised me to write back through the Salvation Army and to include my telephone number, so that's exactly what I did.

One Sunday afternoon, I had been able to get down the stairs to enjoy having time with the family and my middle daughter and I were clearing up after lunch. The 'phone rang. A lady told me that she was the person who had contacted me through the Salvation Army; she told me about my brother and how they had always known he had a full-blood sister out there. They had traced me with the help of investigations by the Salvation Army. I really couldn't believe this and asked how I could know it was genuine, so she read out my brother's birth certificate which indeed showed the same address and mother's and father's names as mine.

At this time there was a programme on TV called 'Surprise, Surprise' hosted by Cilla Black. I just said, "Is Cilla Black going to come in at any moment?" My heart was thumping and I really did not know how to respond. Surely this was wrong – wouldn't my Mum have said something? I asked if I could call her back another time to have a conversation because this had come as a complete surprise to me, then as I put down the 'phone I wept and wept. Never in their lives had any of my children seen me in such despair. I couldn't tell them anything for at least ten minutes.

So many questions were in my mind about this latest revelation. All the pent-up sadness within me seem to burst and I could not believe any of this was happening. That night, alone in my bed, I went through my normal routine of thanking Spirit for being with me and asking for guidance and protection; suddenly an orb came into the room (I didn't know at the time that this is what this bright ball of energy is called). So I knew that Spirit was keeping me safe and all would be well very soon.

They were preparing me for the pathway ahead. Crowfoot told me that 'the brambles' had now been taken away, and my life and work for Spirit must now continue. Meditation is a very good way of making that connection with the spirit world. Never think it is just your imagination when you are spoken to and given information, they just use that part of the brain in order to give you their message. Write it down. Always thank Spirit and be humbled by the gift they have bestowed upon you.

I wept again, still in despair. Despite this reassurance, when were these challenges to end? I really couldn't take any more.

You are stronger than you think

I began writing to my newly-found brother, Ray. I was not yet ready to talk to him in person, it was easier to make that contact via letters. I was also getting myself prepared for major surgery so, all in all, the timing could not have been worse. There was no-one whom I felt I could talk to about my brother except a cousin and my Uncle Sid.

Cousin Jean was only six years younger than my Mum, so I thought she might know exactly what went on during that time. Jean outlined certain things that had happened and Uncle Sid, who was Mum's brother, knew the details. My Mum had been in a relationship with a married man whose wife had refused to divorce him, so my Mum had changed her name by deed poll to my biological father's name.

It seems they had lived as man and wife for some time. Mum gave birth to me and was expecting my brother when my father was involved in a fatal accident. The next of kin was called, who was obviously his wife. Those days were very different to now, no support was given, and indeed my Mum was now classed as a single unmarried mother, a disgrace back then. She couldn't even go to the funeral in Essex, our home being in Birmingham. She must have been devastated and wondering know how she was going to cope financially with two children yet without a partner's support.

My father's widow had not realised there were children involved. When my brother was born, she came for a meeting with my Mum and wanted to take both of us children to look after us. She was the legal widow, with a widow's pension and insurance pay-outs. So financially she would have had the means to do this. Saying this, she also had four children of her own to take care of, so this was really charitable and caring of her. She must have been a strong and determined person. Here was her husband's mistress, yet she was willing to bring up his children by this woman.

After much heart-searching, my mother decided to let my brother go with her at the age of six weeks, but kept me by her side. Maybe it was because, at the age of two, my personality was already part of her life, I don't know. But when I was three and a half she then decided that it would be better for me to be placed in a children's home. It took a long time for me to forgive that action, especially after my brother made himself known to me. I revisited my childhood memories and had to deal with the emotion all over again.

My stepfather, bless him, knew nothing about the existence of my brother and I was determined that he would never need to know until it was necessary. My two sisters were also kept in the dark initially because I was still stunned by the whole business.

I wanted to get to know the man who was my brother and so we exchanged photographs and letters for some time. Looking at the photographs of him, I was amazed by how alike we were. He also sent me a picture of our biological father and again the likeness was uncanny. (Although I look very much like my Mum, I am the image of my maternal grandmother.) I explained that I was about to go into surgery and it would be better to keep the communication going this way until all that was over. He was quite willing to go at my pace and slowly we built up this long-distance sibling relationship. One ironic thing was that his daughter was born on the same date as my middle daughter, although a few years apart. It seemed we had the same sense of humour and he really wanted to get to know me. He had apparently promised his Mum that he would find me; well, he didn't acknowledge his biological mother as his Mum, but a mother's love can come from the bond formed throughout the years and not solely from biology. She really was his Mum and had taken care of him. Now she had died, he remembered his promise and decided to find me.

The Queen once called a certain year her 'annus horribilis' and, believe you me, this was that type of year for me. I was afraid that something else would come along and take the rug from beneath my feet.

But once again I was reassured by a medium from the rostrum at the church. Val had insisted I go with her, she even said, "I know you will have a message tonight." She was such a good friend to me, and would often come to the rescue when things were very difficult. I was due to go into hospital the following week and, to be honest, with all that was going on I was looking at this as a chance for some 'time out'!

This message was from my granddad, telling me that healing was coming my way in abundance and I was not to worry because they would strengthen me for my work, which needed to be done. It seemed incredible, I shook my head and was almost in tears. How on Earth was I going to carry on with anything? I didn't even know what the outcome of the operation would be.

But then the medium also told me about a man called Joe and my ears pricked up because this was my real father's name. He was with me, she said, and had watched events unfold in the last few weeks. Now tears did run down my face.

"You are stronger than you think," he said. "This is not a test of endurance and you will never look back. This moment is a turning point. And I am glad you are together again. Keep faith." The message was so thought-provoking. Joe also said that it had 'all started in Winchester'. I couldn't relate to this information but decided I would try to find out what he meant.

A few days later I called my Uncle Sid, whose health hadn't been too good lately. He was the oldest of three siblings, one of whom was my Mum who had recently gone to spirit along with my Auntie Lil, who had been gone for several years. I told him about my message and asked him if he knew what was meant by the reference to 'Winchester'. Uncle Sid explained that Winchester was the town where Mum and Joe had made their first home together. Once again, this was profound evidence of spirit communication because I'd had no knowledge at all of those events.

He also said that it was almost my time to 'take over', but he was hanging on until I was ready. Again, I laughed down the 'phone and said, "Uncle Sid, you'll have to hang on for a long time yet, it will take me ages to start serving churches again." He just said, "We'll see."

Indeed, we shall see, I thought, my mind racing. I had no idea where I would be in the future; apparently, only Spirit was privy to that information.

A NEW LIFE BEGINS

My operation was a success and no further treatment was needed. Due to my MS and recovery from surgery, my eldest daughter offered me a place to stay for the short term. She had a downstairs toilet and made her dining room into a bedroom for me because I was unable to use the stairs. I had a dread of returning home, of course, because I had started divorce proceedings and was told by our Housing Association that they could not rehouse me until the divorce was finalised. This seemed really unfair so I was inspired to write to my local councillor. Out of the blue, I had a visit from someone in the Housing Department who assessed my needs and asked whether I was willing to give up my share of the tenancy of the house I had lived in with my husband. Naturally, my answer was a definite "Yes!", and to my astonishment the offer of a ground floor flat was made a week later.

My youngest daughter had by now gone off to university; my dog of many years had had to be put down after she suffered a stroke; I was going through a divorce; I had been diagnosed with MS and cancer in the same year; and I had moved to a new house. But when I shut the front door of my own new little palace it was wonderful. I loved that little flat. There had been a smoker in the place previously, so with the help of my lovely family we stripped walls, cleaned and painted and got it into a liveable condition. I moved in with an old settee given by my youngest sister and a mattress on the floor. The only furniture I had brought with me was a dresser and table and chairs from the house.

I was now alone for the first time in many years and although sometimes I felt lonely I also had a sense of peace. As I sat on the settee in my new home, a feeling of contentment was flowing through me. But... I had no money left. I had paid all my bills and I only had three slices of bread to eat, nothing else. I had no money to feed myself. Then the telephone rang. It was one of the committee members of Bromsgrove Spiritualist Church.

"Pam, would you do us a favour?" she asked. "There's someone in real need who could do with a private sitting."

"Oh," I hesitated, "I've never done a private sitting – am I good enough for that? I wouldn't know how to approach it."

"Pam, you are ready. Your name came into my mind the moment the lady asked. You can use the church and I will be there too, cleaning. You can take her into the little room and Spirit will be with you. Please say 'yes'," was the reply.

"Of course, especially if the lady is in dire need," I said. So arrangements were made. I was told that I should charge the going rate, to be split between me and the church. Now I had the means to feed myself for a little while. Furthermore, it was a valuable show of faith in me, not only from Bromsgrove Spiritualist Church but from Spirit too.

The lady's husband came through, I mentioned him by name and described his character. He reminded her of something that had happened which had made them both laugh: she had a holiday snap of her daughter in her Dad's huge wellingtons when she was a little girl.

The lady was in tears. She was given reassurance that her husband was now out of pain and watching over everyone on the Earth, especially their daughter and grandchild. I was also able to tell her that she would receive 'a sign' from her husband shortly, and then she would know for sure that he was around.

This lady had lost her husband very recently to cancer; her daughter had just been diagnosed with it as well, then the family had another bitter blow in that a grandchild had leukaemia. A couple of months later I spoke with the lady at church. She told me that her daughter's cancer had been caught early enough to suggest a good prognosis and the grandchild was also responding well to treatment.

She actually laughed when telling me about the 'sign' her husband had given her. When he died, the family had searched everywhere for the key to the garden shed as they wanted to sort it out; but the key could not be found so the lock was broken and her son had to replace it. One morning recently she was hanging washing out in the garden when she noticed that one of the plant pots outside the shed door had toppled over. Lo and behold, underneath it was the key to the shed door. Some may say that this is 'just coincidence', but she had been told to expect a sign and Spirit works in mysterious ways!

Soon, my new life had begun and I threw myself into my spiritual work in a big way. I was now booked for several churches around the Midlands area and I was asked to do days of readings and 'psychic suppers'. During my meditations, I was given a lot of information and began to trust Spirit's wisdom more than ever.

Uncle Sid had been taken ill and was in hospital. When I went to see him he eyed me seriously and said, "Do not ever let the ego become you – as Spirit give they can take it away. So always be thankful that you are the instrument of Spirit." Not long after this he died. I have tried to live by his words ever since.

Often, as clairvoyants, we are called on to predict the next love in people's lives, as though we are some sort of 'Love Island Medium'!

Sometimes I have even been asked during such readings what colour hair the next boyfriend or girlfriend will have. I accept this as part of what people think that being psychic or clairvoyant means, though it is not what the connection with Spirit is all about. Still, we are all hankering for some indications of our future life in some way, so I don't blame those who want to know. (Mind you, as I often say, if I had known what was going to happen around the corner in my own life I would have walked the other way!)

On one occasion, a young girl came for a reading expecting me to tell her who her next boyfriend would be. However, during the session her granddad came through with information she couldn't really understand at the time, but he insisted that he needed to talk to her mother. A tape recording of the reading was made and the girl promised that she would play it to her Mum, but said, "I don't think she'll come but we'll see what she says." I smiled, gave her a hug, and knew that if Spirit wanted me to see her Mum then somehow it would be arranged.

A couple of days afterwards the `phone rang, and it was the young girl making an appointment for her Mum. What had persuaded her to do this? Well, when the tape was played, the girl's granddad's voice was clearly heard calling her Mum's name! This had not been heard in the room during our session, and it was a wonderful way for the gentleman to make sure his daughter came for a message. This turned out to be very profound and, indeed, in some respects changed the course of his daughter's life. Once again, Spirit showed the way.

I had happily been serving the churches again for over twelve months when I was approached by a lady who ran a church in Stafford, asking me to do a workshop for them. This was in the days when Stafford Church met in a rented space above a wine shop. This lady almost demanded that I do the workshop. I was flabbergasted and hesitated to give an answer, but she said, "They have told me you are to start teaching others. Your gift is to pass the word on to others of like mind." She watched my face intently, then went on to say, "My guide is telling me your tough life has prepared you so that nothing will daunt you, nothing will hold you back. However, beware of jealously and betrayal by those who purport to be spiritual.

"You have your diary," she smiled and patted my arm, "so we'll make a date now and you can let me know what you want to do so I can prepare the people for the workshop. You are not to refuse me, this is the word of Spirit, so in essence you have no choice."

I was astonished! I had indeed got my diary with me and we made a date. Still, I was so taken aback that on my way home that night I spoke to Spirit in the car and said, "How can I teach when I am still learning?"

"Because we know you are ready," was the answer.

I was inspired to create the content of the workshop by Crowfoot. I remember that it was a particularly bad night in winter when I arrived; it had started to snow just as I got to the venue, so my anxiety was not only for this very first workshop, but the journey home along the motorway was also on my mind. There were several people there and this lovely lady made me welcome. When I had finished, she told me that this was the start of many workshops for me and apparently everyone had enjoyed it so much they'd asked her to book me again.

Life was beginning to feel better and I was still attending my local church whenever I was not serving other churches. Val would come with me on my journeys and we would have many a laugh in the car about this and that. She had now divorced and begun working as a warden for sheltered housing. We kept each other going in a way, crying on each other's shoulders and laughing at each other's antics. Val encouraged me to start living again, as I stimulated her to do the same. Spiritually, she was still a believer but she knew that her real job was done: she was the one who opened the doors and set the process going for me. And she opened another door for me when she introduced me to her sister's ex-husband, Don. Val and I had known each other a long time, our children had grown up together and I had fleetingly seen Don when he had called on Val with his children. We seemed to hit it off.

So now I began dating again. Val had also met someone, a milkman where she worked, and they were planning to move away down south together to work as warden and gardener at a sheltered housing complex in Henley-on-Thames. It was an idyllic job for them to get together. I 'phoned when I could and went down to see her as often as possible. Our friendship was something that would be sustained no matter what and whatever the distance was between us.

Tragedy

Val's daughter Emma was having marriage problems and Val had asked if she could come up and stay for a couple of days. Her partner Derek stayed behind because someone needed to take on the responsibilities of warden while Val was gone. She just wanted to see her family and reassure her daughter that she was there for her.

We were chatting and catching up when the 'phone rang at about 9.15 p.m. Suddenly, a great feeling of doom came upon me. When I answered, it was Val's daughter saying that she had come back from night school to find the house in darkness and her husband and children missing. On the dining table, all their insurance policies were laid out. She was crying hysterically.

"I know he's done something awful," she kept saying. Val tried to calm her and said we would be there in five minutes. She put the 'phone down and immediately rang the police to meet us at her daughter's house.

The trauma of that night will live with me forever. A policewoman stayed with us and several police were out looking for Val's son-in-law and her grandchildren, a boy aged five and a girl aged seven. Their school bags were still in the living room, swimming gear still wet discarded in the kitchen. All I could do was comfort them both and we waited seemingly for hours for news of where they were. Somehow, I knew even before we got to the house that something was terribly wrong. Val turned to me and asked, "Do you feel a foreboding?" I couldn't speak, just nodded. We had always been truthful with one another so I couldn't bear pretending to be hopeful, I just gave her a hug. What more can you do in these circumstances?

Don arrived (he was Emma's uncle) and Val's son also came. I seemed to be in the kitchen making endless cups of tea just to keep my mind occupied and give support by quietly getting on with the mundane. The atmosphere was thick with tension and anxiety, the waiting interminable. Just past midnight I heard the police radio come to life and the policewoman went outside into the garden; but I heard the words, "Alright, I will try to have a word with the mother."

My heart sank. They had found the car; the husband had taken the children and used a pipe attached from the exhaust into the car and gassed them all. I wept and didn't know how Val and her family were ever going to face life again. It seems that the husband was a controlling sort of man and had planned this for some days, since they had decided that the marriage would end. He had written in a note left in the car that, if he could not have the children, then Emma wasn't having them either. It was a vengeful, spiteful act in which two innocent children's lives were taken.

I held Val in my arms more than once after all this and we cried on each other's shoulders. Emma was numb and it was only after the funerals had come and gone that she started to respond to life again, but it was very hard for her. Of course, she also had to arrange her husband's funeral, the last thing she wanted to do under such terrible circumstances. At the children's funeral, seeing two small white coffins side by side was so heart-wrenching. Words cannot express how one would feel as a mother, losing two children in such a dreadful way. The police were wonderful though, escorting the funeral cortege to and from the crematorium. Val was heartbroken, she had lost her lovely grandchildren and kept asking, "Why?"

"I can't tell you, Val, I wish I had an answer," I told her one day. "I just know that your Mum is looking after them and you will hear from them very soon." Yet in my heart I knew that she would never, ever, forget the chain of events that happened during this time.

Our faith is tested quite a lot during our pathway through life and this instance gave mine a short, sharp shock. I questioned my guide, Crowfoot, as to why this kind of thing was allowed to happen; but all I was told was that some things are beyond any reasoning. The one who had done this was a human being with his own frailties and who didn't listen to guidance. Our guides and our guardian angels can only look on and help by giving us a push here and there – but they cannot live our lives for us. Even when something so huge impacts us, they can only watch and wait to see how we deal with it and then give support where it is needed.

Personally, I do believe that we live several lives before deciding to stay in the spirit world. When I teach, I offer the analogy of an orange being the soul and each segment of the orange is a lifetime. When we return to the soul, we take with us what we have learned in this lifetime and then we bring elements of those lifetimes and experiences with us when we come back. How many of us go to a place and feel that we have been there before? Or maybe we meet a person and we feel we have known them for years. These people may have been 'on the same orange tree' as us and are often the people we have a real affinity with in this lifetime; others we meet may be 'in the same orange grove', and although we may get on with them we don't necessarily have the same kind of bond.

I am only human and have human frailties, so I could not offer a reason why that man had decided he would take his children with him. But I do believe in retribution for our actions either here on Earth or in the spirit world, and I also know he would have been prevented from being with his children in the spirit world. Maybe this would have been his 'punishment'.

There is, I'm sure, a purpose for us to be here; it may take a lifetime to find that purpose and fulfil it, whilst some people must live several lifetimes in order to gain a real insight into their purpose. I have gleaned my own purpose this time and I only hope that I will live long enough to fulfil my service to Spirit, engaged in teaching and mentoring several people before I return home to the spirit world.

DEVELOPMENTS

My mentor and friend, Anne Taylor, struck a deal with me that we would go down to serve Stroud and Cirencester Spiritualist churches together. The services were on Friday and Saturday evenings; if she was working, I would go with her and vice versa. We stayed overnight at the home of the president of the churches, which was an old school house in a small village. We had such a warm welcome and our stays were always filled with laughter as well as spiritual enhancement.

One evening when we had returned from church, it was decided that we would 'sit and send energy' whilst allowing Ken, the president, to go into trance. This house was not disturbed by street lighting, only the light from passing cars came into the room when all the house lights were out and this didn't happen very often because it was a very secluded area. This winter's night, Ken's wife Freda wrapped us up in scarves and put blankets over our knees, and we sat in anticipation of Ken going into trance.

Suddenly, I saw an orb arrive seemingly through the window and hover over Ken's seat. This came as a car passed by, so I thought maybe it was light from the car. Anne hadn't been aware of it at all and at first I put it down to my imagination. As the evening wore on, Ken's face completely changed. His words were very profound and we were even able to ask some questions, which were answered very precisely. I was astounded. This was fantastic – although I had seen trance before, this seemed especially powerful. Then, as Ken was coming round, this orb appeared to rise to the ceiling and go out of the window; this time, Anne and Freda both saw it happen. We spoke with Ken afterwards and he agreed that it did seem to feel a lot more potent this time. When you see this phenomenon and realise that it can only come from the spirit world, it makes you feel humble and more curious about what is next.

And there was more to come. The next day, I was serving the church and from the rostrum a message came for Ken about his work for Spirit. This was going to change but he would find it much better because 'someone was coming to help' with the task. The information came with facts about his guide and only Ken would be able to identify with this. Afterwards he told me, "Well done," which was praise indeed from him. His work did change and he became an important figure in the south-west Spiritualist movement. He has since gone to the spirit world, but I know that he would have been determined for the work go on for the benefit of all.

I had a request for a reading from a gentleman who was in a great deal of distress and in fact was going through a bad time with depression and ill-health. When we had almost finished the reading, I was told by Crowfoot, "You need to do some healing on him." I questioned this at the time because I had never done healing. Well, it depends on what is meant by healing – talking and listening can be very much part of the healing process and this is what I try to do in my sessions. I asked the gentleman if he was willing for me to do some healing on him, which he agreed to, so we began to change the room around to accommodate this.

I was guided by Spirit during the process and became aware of a beautiful angelic presence that was so powerful. Afterwards, we discussed how this presence had filled the room with light even though we both had our eyes closed at this point. The gentleman felt elated and uplifted and was able to feel hopeful; something had shifted for him during this healing process and would stay with him. He gave me a hug and said he would never forget this, that it had given him a reason to keep going.

As we shifted back the furniture, underneath his chair was a white feather. It had not been there before! We had shifted all the furniture to accommodate the procedure so we both knew that it had come during the healing. Again, a sign that meant a great deal to me but, more to the point, to the person who received that healing. Months later I had a 'phone call from the man; once again he thanked me and said that his life was back to normal now but the start of his recovery was when he had come to me and the marvellous healing he'd received. He'd moved too far away to come to see me again, but he was getting healing on a regular basis from somebody who practised Reiki and he knew it was doing him good. This was meant to be. Again, Spirit had opened a door and he began to realise that this had been a sign for him to continue believing in healing and in the spiritual energy that can be received.

I started to meet up on a regular basis with two lovely friends of mine, Yvette and Linzi. We would gather at Yvette's house and meditate together. Linzi had a great interest in spiritual things and in astrology, and Yvette is a healer who has inspired many people during her work for Spirit.

During this time, I had become very much aware of the presence of 'Abraham'. He had made himself known to me during my quiet contemplation at home and sometimes in dreams. One day, our little group went into meditation and I went very deeply into trance. I was aware of Abraham coming very close and, indeed, for the first time he began to speak through me to Linzi and Yvette.

His philosophy and words were very profound. He began with the words, "I am the word. I am the light. I am known by many names, but you will call me Abraham." He came with healing for the world and warned that the time had come for changes that mankind would benefit from; but there needed to be a shift in how the world leaders would come together. This was the first of many times that Abraham would speak through me. When he speaks, he has a very dominant male voice and it surprised me that I was able to do the trance phenomenon in this way. It was obviously time now for me to be inspired by this evolved spirit. The first time it happened I was amazed because it had never been my intention for this to occur; and subsequently, when it does happen, it will often take place at unexpected times. It was another new development in my spiritual work that would enhance and stimulate my gift for future work on behalf of Spirit.

I soon became very busy, with several bookings for the next couple of years. I was being asked to do quite a few workshops and it seemed that more and more people had a curiosity about spiritual things. Two very good friends of mine, Sue and John, began doing Psychic Shows providing talks, private readings, healing, alternative therapies and workshops; for a small charge, visitors could experience the whole day. I was asked to participate and I remember saying to Sue and John, "I'll take my book and a newspaper in case no-one wants a reading."

Today there are many such shows about but back then it was a new venture. No-one could have anticipated the impact such shows had, not only on the visitors but also on those who provided the therapies and healing. In fact, the interest was phenomenal and many people came; it was especially thought-provoking how many people had an interest in all spiritual subjects. I did several readings, a workshop and a talk, all of which seemed to go well. My friends Sue and John often laugh about that first show. They made it look easy to organise but I know it wasn't; not all shows have the right mix of people but these did. Anne and I would subsequently join in with these shows and go together to do our work.

My personal life began to become more content and life seemed much calmer. I finally started to meet up with my new-found brother and his wife and children. Don and I were seeing each other on a regular basis and enjoying our time together. My youngest daughter was still at university and my other daughters were more settled in their lives. The spiritual work became the focus of my life. Don would sometimes come to venues with me, but often I would go on my own to serve the churches, which I would enjoy immensely. I always felt that if I had helped one person in the audience then that is what I was meant to do.

During this time, I meditated as often as I could and my relationship with Crowfoot was becoming stronger. I realised that I had begun to have the trust with him that I had heard other mediums have with their guides.

Then, much later, my close friend Joan gave me a book all about Crowfoot's life on Earth and it would be good to pass on some of this to you here. Crowfoot was born in 1830 into the Crow tribe. When his father died, his mother married a brave from the Blackfoot tribe, to which Crowfoot gave his allegiance. He became a perceptive, far-seeing chief who was a diplomat, establishing good relations with fur traders and peace with the Cree tribe. In 1874, Crowfoot welcomed the Canadian government agencies when they came to stamp out the whisky trade. He knew this had had a bad impact on his people and he wanted to stop them getting drunk and losing sight of what was important, thus keeping the tribe together. He was recognised as an ally and given a prominent role in the Treaty No. 7 negotiations in 1877.

After the Blackfoot settled on their reservation in 1881, Crowfoot became disillusioned with the government but refused to allow his people to join the 1885 North-West Rebellion, less out of loyalty to the government than from the belief that it was a losing battle. Sick during his last decade, he constantly mourned the loss of his children, of whom only one blind son and three daughters reached maturity. Near death, he is quoted as saying, "What is life? It is the flash of a firefly in the night. It is the breath of a buffalo in the winter time. It is as the little shadow that runs across the grass and loses itself in the sunset." He died in 1890, aged 60.

One evening, I was told by Crowfoot, "You need to learn at a place of greater knowledge and gain a piece of paper to prove your expertise." I jotted this information down in my book and subconsciously was watching out for the signpost that would show me the way. Months passed and all the spiritual pathways I had assumed could be the way forward were closed or were held on days when I had a venue already booked in my diary. Then, one very wet morning, the local newspaper arrived through the letterbox completely sodden. I laid it on the worktop in my kitchen to dry out and saw, as I spread it out, that the page it was opened at carried the prospectus of the local college. Advertised there was a course in 'the competency of teaching', which ran for a year. I had a shiver up and down my spine as I knew this was what I had to do. However, I worried about the cost and whether I was capable of the task before me.

A telephone conversation with the college reassured me about the cost, as I was able to fund it by three payments, so that box was ticked. The course allowed mature students to attend without recent qualifications, the only proviso being that I had to be able to show that I was doing some sort of teaching at the time. I asked Bromsgrove Spiritualist Church if they would allow me to do some workshops there; after discussing the reason for my request and what these workshops would involve, they supported my request, for which I was very grateful.

So here was the next new chapter opening for me. Although I had done many workshops by now, the course gave me insights into how to time the lessons and how to judge whether the students were learning and enjoying the course. The curious thing about all this was that, in order to assess my teaching, I had to invite my tutor to the Spiritualist church. She was very sceptical and, I sensed, afraid of what was in store for her. My workshop at the time was called "Who am I"? My tutor explained the process of assessment: she would come and sit at the back of the room and make notes, then leave after about half an hour.

I was very nervous, but having started teaching I just forgot that I was being assessed. The students, including my tutor, had been given a handout with a few pertinent questions for them to think about and to answer on the paper; we would discuss these afterwards. This process highlighted lots of quite deep and meaningful issues for people, examining their own thoughts for the first time. I always finish my teaching with a short meditation and by reading a spiritual enlightenment card with words that would help them for the next week. My tutor was still there at the end. She was so entranced and this was the first time she had meditated in her life! She found the whole process enriching and my assessment went very well indeed.

I passed the course and the tutor wanted me to carry on so I could take the next stage; but I had done what I set out to do. I was not going to teach a curriculum to school children. The course gave me a qualification for my teaching skills so that I could pass on my knowledge to others. Little did I realise what this would mean for the future of my workshops.

A POSITIVE TURN

Another wonderful event that year was that Don and I became engaged. My youngest daughter was graduating from university later in the year so we decided to wait to get married until our daughters were more settled. We had also not moved in together because of that. Don's daughter was living with him since his ex-wife had decided she could no longer cope when their daughter was just eleven years old; but now, at twenty-one, she was ready to spread her wings and become more independent.

My daughter came home and started work, and had decided to buy our council flat. A housing trust was taking over all the properties and before this took effect the council was offering to sell them off to sitting tenants at a percentage of their value. We discussed this at length and it seemed a good way for her to get onto the property ladder with a postgraduate mortgage. The idea was that I would pay rent to her and the place would be hers to revamp for herself.

Don and I now decided to set a date for our wedding, for the following year. My daughter seemed to be settled and we were in the process of getting his daughter settled as well. At long last, life seemed to be taking on a much better view.

I carried on doing my workshops and spiritual work serving the churches. During one of these workshops, again for my very good friends Sue and John, a lady attended who taught at a local college. When the workshop finished she asked whether I would be interested in taking this into the college. I hesitated, firstly because I had never thought of this as a subject that the college would have an interest in, and then also because of my self-doubt again. Was this where I needed to be and was I capable of it? But the words came out of my mouth without my even thinking about them, "Of course, I would love to do that."

Spirit again worked their magic and this lady became a friend who had lots to tell me and show me. True to her word, she approached the college and the person in charge of recreational courses called me a few days later to make an appointment to see me. She asked me to bring in the curriculum I would follow, say how many weeks it would be and which nights I could be available.

I was amazed but terrified! What did I have to offer? So for a couple of weeks I worked on developing a six-week curriculum. Presenting to the college administrator turned out to be quite easy. She told me that a new ruling was coming in and all part-time teachers would have to sit the '7307 course' to prove their suitability for teaching; would I be willing to undertake this course? I smiled and showed her my certificate. Spirit had given me a nod in the right direction again: she was extremely pleased with this and proceeded to tell me the date we would start, expressing the need for at least seven people to attend before they could consider running the course. So I said to Spirit, "If you need me to teach this course, you need to send the people." That plea was answered. Two days after the enrolment started a 'phone call from the college astounded me – they asked whether I could possibly offer two days because there were seventeen people enrolled and nineteen more wanted to come! The answer was obviously 'Yes'. After the first six weeks, I was asked if I wanted to continue the course, and whether I would be able to come up with another six-week curriculum for the next term; moreover, if the interest carried on, would I do a further six-week curriculum the following term? This made a full syllabus of eighteen weeks in total. This response was incredible, so many people were beginning to crave more information as they had experiences they wanted to have explained.

During my teaching, I gained lots of insights into many things and to information from Spirit that came in unexpected ways. One year, I had two pairs of mother-and-daughter students. One pair had a great deal of spiritual awareness and the daughter of the other duo was an agnostic; she had come just out of curiosity with her Mum, who read Tarot cards for her friends and wanted to have a bit more knowledge. When the class introduced themselves, the agnostic daughter expressed her view of not believing in anything but wanting to be proved wrong. This set off a debate within the class, led by the other mother-and-daughter pair who were disgusted that anyone could come to a class like this with views that were so contrary to their own. I diplomatically told the class that all views were accepted and tolerance was a very spiritual thing… This maintained an uneasy peace between the two pairs.

During the class, my way of getting people into pairs was to put some playing cards into a dish for the students to pick out. Each person would pair up with the matching card, for example, two red fives. This meant that the choices were random. During the first six-week course, somehow inevitably, the duos of mothers and daughters were paired together and began to understand one another better. The agnostic daughter told me that the course had changed her mind and her curiosity was satisfied; she did not continue with the course but thanked me for opening her eyes. Spirit work in marvellous ways.

Another time, a gentleman told me that he was out to prove there was absolutely nothing in what I claimed to be true. He was going to document it all and prove me wrong. Did this daunt me? No! I know without any doubt that Spirit exists and that we can communicate with them if they so wish. I also know that I do not 'call them up'. I use my gift with love and caring, with great respect and responsibility. This is one of the things I teach and say on a regular basis. Whenever we use our spiritual gifts, we must always remember to use them with loving care and responsibility.

The gentleman signed up for the first six weeks. My first week was all about the aura and the colours within the auric field. I asked the students to take a pair of divining rods, move towards the partner they had paired up with and watch as the rods either drew together or moved wider apart. This would show where the edge of the auric field was. This gentleman just scoffed at the idea of anyone having an aura. So when his rods started to move he was aghast and kept saying they must be rigged. And throughout the six weeks he kept shaking his head with disbelief.

Sometimes the students would be asked to use clairvoyance and give each other little messages. The messages my sceptical gentleman received from these strangers amazed him; but, most of all, his messages for them startled him. He could not believe himself capable of such things. He came to me at the end of the six weeks and shook my hand.

"It will lead me to research all of this," he said. "Most of all, I apologise for my arrogance of non-belief." He didn't come for the rest of the course but I knew that he had been shown enough, and maybe he would impart what he had gleaned to others and get them thinking in a different way. This is what we can do – plant the seed and then the tree will grow strong and mighty with knowledge and trust. I have knowledge but I would never expect all others just to believe;

it is entirely up to the individual to have their own belief and develop their own awareness. As we often say, there is more to Heaven and Earth than we know…

Messages from beyond

During the years of doing private readings, I have had many an interesting experience with clients but I usually do not get to hear any more about the reading until someone calls me or comes to see me again.

On one occasion, I did a reading for a lady and spoke of a link very close to her that was in America; she would come to know about this after the September of that year. She was told this by her father who was in the spirit world. He also wanted her to 'be prepared'. Although the lady could not relate at all to this at the time, she assumed her father was talking about being prepared for her mother's passing.

After each reading, I supply a tape recording. I know that so much information comes through that often the client will not remember it all, even if they start to make notes; they get transfixed on what I am saying so don't write down all the information given. Well, a few months later the lady listened to her tape again and was so flabbergasted by the information I'd given her that she called me up to discuss it.

Her mother had indeed passed away, so as an only child she had the task of sorting out the house and contents. Up in the attic, she had found a box containing photographs of a baby boy and some letters, including a letter of adoption; the correspondence also stated that the couple who had adopted the boy had moved to America. It transpired that the lady's parents had been only fourteen and fifteen at the time and had been forced by their own parents to give up their little boy. The mother had written a history of these events for anyone who found the box and had even stressed the need to find the little boy, as he was a brother to the children she would go on to have later.

The lady in fact then found her brother and began to have contact with him, although it was very uneasy in the beginning. She thanked me again for the information I had given her. I related to her my experience of finding my own brother and tried to reassure her, since part of my role as a medium is to counsel and uplift the client. This role carries such responsibility and I always try not to let the ego rule. When such feedback comes to confirm what Spirit has said, it always gives me comfort to know that they are watching over us.

But a great blow for me at this time was that Val became very ill, having complained about pains in her lower back and tummy for some time. The doctor kept saying that this was due to Post-Traumatic Stress Disorder, because of what had happened to her daughter and grandchildren. She was losing weight and I insisted she should go back to the doctor and ask for a second opinion. Her family and I were all worried about her. She took my advice and several tests later they discovered that she had pancreatic cancer, which by now had gone too far to be treated.

I was inconsolable for several days after this. But I realised how selfish this was, because Val needed people around her to give her support, not wailing at the thought of it all. Her son had booked his wedding for the following year and this kept Val going, so determined was she that she would attend this wedding. I tried to visit her whenever I could and, a month before she died, I gave her future daughter-in-law a lift home. She asked whether I thought Val would make it to the wedding next year or they should bring it forward. I looked her straight in the eye and just said it would have to be arranged very quickly, because I didn't think she would be here for Christmas of that year (it was now the middle of November). Her daughter stayed with her in the final weeks and I only saw her once more before she passed. Her funeral was a few days before Christmas. Her daughter said that she knew her mother was at peace now and, somehow, she felt better about the children because she knew Val would be looking after them.

Several days later, I had a vivid dream in which Val was on a lovely white beach; the sun was shining, the sea was calm, and she had the two children either side of her. When she turned to see me, she waved. I woke up and wrote all this down with the intention of telling her daughter; when I did so she smiled and nodded. Tears came for both of us, and we knew Val would have somehow tried to make us laugh if she had been with us, to stop the tears.

The following year, Val's son invited Don and me to their wedding. Once there, he related the story of a spiritual happening on the morning of the wedding. Val had always told me that if I saw a magpie around it was her; this related back to the time her Mum had died, when several magpies were around as she was cremated. Val had believed this to be a sign of her Mum's presence. This morning, on Val's son's lawn, had stood an adult magpie with two young ones: this was Val and the two grandchildren, come to say 'Hello and best of luck'. They'd come right up to the patio doors and seemed to look in, so I do think Val's son was right. It would have been just her style, and she had been determined to be there at the wedding. How often do we see baby magpies?

For some time afterwards, whenever I saw a magpie and I hadn't heard from Val's daughter in a while, it would spur me on to call her and ask how she was. Invariably it would transpire she was having a tough time.

No matter what you think of these signs, they come from Spirit to give us reassurance that they are always with us. We must look for the signs and watch out for things we might call 'coincidence'. Really, it is Spirit giving us encouragement.

Don and I decided to get married in Gretna Green, a famous place on the borders of England and Scotland. In days gone by, the age of consent was lower in Scotland than anywhere else in the British Isles, so young couples would elope and get married over the blacksmith's anvil.

We wanted to involve only our immediate family, just our girls and grandchildren who were all bridesmaids or page boys; my eldest daughter gave me away and my youngest was Don's 'best man'. It was a second marriage for both of us so, although we wanted to keep it low key, it also had to be a special time for us both. However, my sisters and my new brother wanted to get involved as well so we had to find suitable overnight accommodation for everyone.

We set out early one Saturday with the intention of finding a suitable place. I had made all the arrangements either by telephone or letter, so this would give us a chance to see where the marriage ceremony would take place and to finalise the arrangements. We approached the Tourist Information Bureau and the assistant there was lovely. When we told her what we wanted she suddenly produced from underneath the counter the brochure of a converted chapel, divided up into small self-catering apartments.

"This has only just come in. The couple have just renovated the building and want to let the apartments," she said with a twinkle in her eye. "It seems such a coincidence that you came in today." She gave me the brochure, which had a contact address and telephone number, so we promptly rang and made an appointment to view the place. When we arrived at the landlord's home, there were wind chimes and statues of angels in the garden, and inside the house there were several crystals on show in various places. I knew this was the place for us.

They were lovely people and even had a limousine for taking everyone to the wedding venue. The wedding day was lovely and Don and I stayed on for a week as our honeymoon.

During this time, we decided to tour around and go to various venues in the area. There was a place called Sweetheart Abbey, where the heart of a knight was said to be placed in a grave within the hall of the small medieval castle. I felt as if I knew this place already, as though I had been there before perhaps in a previous lifetime, and I pointed out the layout without us having to read the various plaques on the walls. Indeed, during this visit I knew that a spirit lady was with me, sharing information that I related to Don as we were going around. Don knew my work for Spirit was important and he listened; I can't say he always understood what I was saying, but knew that the evidence would come afterwards.

I began to jot it all down, so enamoured was I about the evidence I was receiving. The lady told me about 'her beloved' John, and that they were together in the spirit world now as they had been in life. She had given this building in memory of him. I was mesmerised. And as I've said before, when Spirit have something to say, they will bring the sign to us and we must believe in what we are getting. Take a notebook around with you: it might be that you will be given information that will be confirmed by doing research later, and this way nothing is forgotten. Spirit will always give it in a way that informs and enlightens us. Indeed, my research afterwards did reveal a wonderful love story and maybe I was given this because, after all, Don and I were honeymooners at the time.

This is the research I found:

"The story of the founding of Sweetheart Abbey is held to be a testament to the enduring power of love. On 10th April, 1273, Lady Devorgilla signed a charter establishing a new Cistercian abbey here in memory of her husband, John Balliol, who had died in 1268. Thanks to the Reformation, her later endowment of a college at Oxford University in his name turned out to be a more enduring memorial.

"Lady Devorgilla's love for her departed husband extended to carrying his embalmed heart around with her in an ivory box with enamelled silver trimmings. After her death in 1290 she was buried in the sanctuary of the abbey church she had founded, and on her instructions the casket containing her husband's heart was buried beside her." The guide book tells us that in tribute to her love for her husband, the monks in the abbey she had founded chose thereafter to call it Dulce Cor, or Sweetheart Abbey. The enduring power of love, certainly, but to squeamish modern sensibilities this is a love story with a distinctly gruesome edge!

Sometimes Spirit take us by surprise. Why we were drawn there? Well, I had been wondering a few days before whether Spirit would want me to carry on in their service, now that my life had changed so much. But I wasn't ready to give up yet.

ANGELS AND GUIDES

I do have an affinity with Scotland and my first visit there was while I was in the process of getting a divorce. I had moved into my flat and would often meditate to receive direction from Spirit. During one of these moments they had given me the images of a thistle and some tartan; as always, I then asked for material evidence, if I were to make a journey to Scotland. I certainly hadn't got the funds for a holiday so I thought this might just have been imagination on my part. However, later that day on the television there was a documentary about the Highlands of Scotland. Coincidence, you might think. But almost a week later I was shopping in the High Street and saw an advertising campaign outside one of the travel agencies; it highlighted Scotland, with a Scottish piper outside regaling us with the dulcet tones of the bagpipes.

For several days, I kept asking whether they wanted me to go and I kept receiving various visions in return. One of these was of going into an old-fashioned church with wood panelling along one wall and talking to a lady who belonged to the church. Another vision was being by a waterfall and watching as others went over a bridge, but realising I mustn't go there, I had to stay and go somewhere else.

Nearly a fortnight later when I was in the High Street again shopping, and after being given a tartan paper bag to put some goods in from the market, I decided on the spur of the moment that I would go to Scotland on my own. There and then, I spent my rent money on a coach trip that was to be going in three weeks' time.

Spending my rent money was not a thing I would normally ever do and this was a first; even if I had nothing left for food, my bills were always paid. Yet while this was certainly out of character for me, somehow it felt right. I knew that Spirit had tested my determination to follow their lead.

The people on the coach were very friendly and the way it was organised, with a number of trips out, made it a special holiday for me. We stayed in Aberdeen and ventured out to various places from there. If you have never been to Scotland, you must try to make that journey at some time in your life – the scenery is magnificent. I was fortunate to have a couple sitting behind me who were nature lovers and along the way they pointed out the deer, the birds of prey, and the different heathers in full bloom on the hillsides.

On one of the visits we stopped at a very pretty village for a twenty-minute 'tea and wee' break, as the driver called it. As we got off the coach, everyone began walking towards a bridge that was beside a beautiful waterfall. I watched in amazement because it was just like my vision: I knew then that I needed to go along the nearby road instead, with my instinct telling me to look for a church. There were no signposts but at the end of this long road stood a small church with its door wide open, so I stepped inside.

The quiet was wonderful and what took me aback was that the church had been built around a small standing stone, the energy of which was singing around the walls. I felt the presence of a spiritual being too and was told to sit, my guide Crowfoot saying that he was with me and not to worry. I could feel myself changing into a young girl, about thirteen years of age, in rags and with no shoes on my feet, so cold I was shivering. I was told to put my hand on the stone, which I did, and a wonderful healing energy burst through me.

For quite a while I had been sad and miserable, although I was very good at masking it, because so much had happened that I was still reeling from the consequences. Whilst others might not have perceived anything untoward happening, I was very good at putting a brave face towards the world when actually falling apart within. The action of the stone was an energy that I simply cannot describe, it was so very special. It was sent by Spirit to boost me and made me realise that this 'holiday' was all about healing me within, to help me with my spiritual work for the future.

We had many trips out and one day we were free to explore Aberdeen. I slowly walked up the main High Street filled with coffee shops, fashion shops and all the regular retail places you would find in a busy city. But I felt myself being drawn up a side road leading to a church in the middle of its own grounds. The sun was shining and my first thought was I would enjoy sitting in the grounds for a while, to have some peace. However, the choir was practising in the church and on hearing this I quietly entered.

Once again, my vision came true as I recognised the wood pan- elling along one wall, obviously added later in the life of the church. As one walked past, it was divided into small sections creating little rooms at the side of the church. An elderly lady approached me and asked if I would help her get up two steps into one of these rooms. Of course I didn't hesitate and she began to chat with me as if she had known me all her life.

"Won't you stay, just to hear the service, my dear?" she asked.

I hesitated but felt a need to sit with this lady, so I stayed. For some reason, she held my hand throughout the prayers, which were said for sending healing to all those in need. There was a quiet period of contemplation and then a final prayer to send healing to the planet and to those who were in the church that day. When all this was over, the lady let go of my hand.

"God is with you always, my dear," she said. "You must believe, and you will always walk with majesty." Tears welled up, then she became very practical and asked to be helped down the steps. She patted my hand and told me to go and get some afternoon tea and reflect on what had happened.

Let these spiritual beings walk with us always, because they will hold us up in all the moments when we need them. Was this an angel in disguise? I don't know, but the energy from this lady was very strong; it helped me to be calm and I felt the energy of healing flow over me during my time with her. I sat on a bench in the grounds of the church for some time before moving on to get my afternoon tea. I was captivated by what had just happened, my earlier vision coming to life.

I'm sure that angels are real. For example, I have been given many crystals during my journey as a medium and often, when I have been to shows or shops selling crystals and spiritual things, I have been drawn to buy particular crystals that have helped in some way at that time. Once, I was given a rose quartz by a friend for healing and during a deep meditation I asked if I could have a little healing from the spirit world. An angelic presence seemed to come into the room and fill the place with light and an overwhelming feeling of love. When I came back to consciousness again, I noticed that the rose quartz had changed and in one corner was an angel wing, which is still present today.

What was next for me? Only Spirit knew. When I got back from Scotland that time, only on my return journey did I start worrying about how I was going to pay the rent. But I needn't have worried because part of it was paid for by a tax refund that came out of the blue. Synchronicity – or was it Spirit showing me the way?

My spiritual work continued and some of the private readings for which I got feedback also gave me some wonderful moments.

A chap came to see me in a very distressed state. He was around twenty-eight years of age. His friend had recommended me and, although he was a reluctant client, here he was in front of me. He related a story of seeing a so-called clairvoyant when he was about seventeen who told him that his life would be over by the age of twenty-nine, so you can imagine why his distress was heightened. This man had got into all the trouble he could: he didn't have a 'stop button', feeling that he had to live in the fast lane because his life would be short. I was so angry, not with him but at the absolute disregard of responsibility this clairvoyant had had for her client's welfare.

I quickly reassured this gentleman that he was not about to be called over anytime soon. Rather, he was to have a complete change in his life. His grandfather came to tell him to grow up and to begin his life again in the proper way. His grandmother, whom he called Nana, was a person he adored, and she came too with lots of memories; one of these was of giving him a tube of Smarties every time he visited as a little boy, and she would tell him each time that she had saved them just for him. This is exactly what she said, with the image of bringing Smarties to this young man (who was in tears by now). He was told by his Nana that he would have a long life and that she would be very happy to see his children, which would happen very soon. Afterwards, he thanked me, said how much better he felt and that he would ring me up to tell me when he'd met that special girl. I laughed and said I expected an invitation to the wedding!

Many months went by, the 'phone rang and this young man, true to his word, gave me a report on what was happening in his life. He had met someone who was very special and he could see them being together forever; he was also doing well in his new job and had just been promoted. He had got his life together at long last and just wanted to say how grateful he was for my wise words. Since then he has gone on to get married and have two lovely children.

How that 'clairvoyant' had changed his life by being so irresponsible still irks me, but sometimes maybe we need a wake-up call to change our lives. Perhaps he had to get into the trouble he did in order to appreciate what he had later in his life. He also went on to help other youngsters who were heading the same way as himself in his younger days. Along the path we must always remember that we cannot do anything about the past, but we can make the future a better place to be.

Spirit can touch people and enlighten them, even those whom you might assume would have no belief in this sort of thing. On another occasion, a very tall man came, again recommended by one of his family. He told me he was in the police force and he was not expecting anything; indeed, he was a real sceptic. He was only here because a relative had been to see me and his Nan had mentioned him by name then, asking for him to be told that she needed to get a message across to him.

The reading began. His father, who had recently gone to the spirit world, thanked him for 'sorting out the flag' for him, saying that he was so happy on the day his son had managed to get permission. When I said this, the look on my client's face was one of astonishment. His Nan said that the family must remain together and that he must go and see his daughter, because she didn't understand and was suffering; yet, she said, things would be sorted out in the end and he would be happy with the outcome. She also told him that he would change his life when he changed his work.

Again, surprise and disbelief came to his face and he just kept shaking his head. It transpired that his father was a retired soldier and permission was needed to put the British flag on his coffin; this was one of the things my client had sorted out because he knew his Dad would have appreciated it. He had also separated from his wife and daughter, with problems occurring over the visitation rights to see the child. And, yes, he had been thinking of changing his career. So all in all this was such a positive confirmation for him that he left a much happier man.

I am no longer amazed by the messages I get to pass on, because I know they come with much love and support from those in the spirit world. But I am still in awe of things that happen when unexpected pathways get opened up and another journey is shown to us.

Don and I decided to move to a new home and try to buy a bungalow. This was because I had fallen from top to bottom of the stairs in our house; I lost my balance due to the MS, so it became important to find a more suitable place to live. We viewed many places that didn't seem right and we had dismissed the one we eventually moved into several times because of the work that needed to be done to bring it into a decent condition. However, as we sat outside waiting for the estate agent, two magpies sat on the lawn and then moved onto the roof. I knew this was Val was telling me that this was the right house. Also, just at the time we exchanged contracts, a friend was moving from the ground floor annexe of a lovely cottage so we were able to stay there while works were being carried out. We were very happy in that bungalow for ten years and it even offered me a place to prepare for my workshops, in the little office we created. Still, even as we moved in I knew we wouldn't be there forever, although I didn't say anything to Don at the time because of all the work we had done to make it feel like home.

We can see signs in the most unexpected ways and what's important is just recognising them as signs and going with them. We shouldn't try to analyse it all. I have a saying, when I am teaching people to tune into Spirit, "Don't think, just link."

My teaching at the college was still going and giving me some wonderful moments of laughter as well as spiritual enlightenment. One of the weeks includes a session on 'animal guides' and 'power animals' – guides from the animal kingdom in the spirit world. Often they come as healers or with your 'doorkeeper' guide as their helpers, or they come simply to give us a message in animal form.

One class was told to take an animal card from the spread on the table. The cards were face down so that they would be chosen randomly. A student looked at her card, the image of a bat, and laughed saying that this meant she was 'a silly old bat'! Bless this lady, she was going through a particularly tough time and had told me privately that she might have to pull out of the course because of the circumstances around her. However, during the class the meaning of the bat became clear: she would have to wait for changes to come, but the wait would be worthwhile and things would prove to be better in the end. I stressed that whilst we knew this had come from Spirit, she was to watch now for two further signs to be sent… The lady had set her TV to record a particular programme that she wanted to watch when she returned home, but somehow it hadn't recorded this programme and instead there was a documentary on – guess what? – bats. She was astonished. Then next day she decided to search the Internet for more information on power animals when she came across a website offering the opportunity to pick an animal card at random – yes, it was the bat. So, you see, if a message is from Spirit they will confirm it for us.

All the teachers at the college, even part-timers like me, had to be assessed often to make sure their teaching was up to standard and soon it was my turn. I was rather worried about this as the designated week for it to take place was the week I would be teaching all about trance. This is an advanced subject as trance means going into an altered state of consciousness very deeply in order to connect with spirit guides and helpers.

Maybe I need to explain first how our brain wave patterns alter in different states of consciousness, such as during meditation.

Beta waves: 24 – 13 cycles per second (cps)

24+   A state of stress or panic.

13 – 23 The normal waking state of concentration, complex mental activity and random thought.

This normal state can vary during the day. For example, how many people have driven their car 'on automatic pilot' and have got to their destination without remembering the journey? This is because our brain wave patterns are changing randomly.

Alpha waves: 13 – 8 cps

13   Silence and stillness, active passivity; meditation.

11   Problem-solving; awareness of one's own power.

10   Awareness of others; telepathy and hypnologic (sleep) inspiration.

9   Clairvoyance, clairaudience, clairsentience.

8   A deeper inspirational state; light trance.

This band of brain waves is where we are using our psychic awareness. Around 10 – 8 cps is where our altered state of consciousness allows the brain to switch to clairvoyant activity and light trance. These are the waves we have when we are just waking up (the hypnopompic state) or just going off to sleep (the hypnogogic); we often receive messages from the spirit world at these times.

Theta waves: 7 – 4.5 cps

7   Mental creativity; a deep yoga state and a mediumistic control state; a possible loss of awareness.

4 – 5   Dream awareness; deeper mediumistic trance state; physical mediumship.

With these waves, brain activity slows down to enable the state of deep meditation and trance in which experienced mediums can invite

Spirit to link with them and talk through them. (As mentioned before, physical mediumship is a unique talent only used by some very experienced mediums.)

Delta waves: 4 – 3 cps

4 – 3   Sleep and loss of consciousness.

So deep trance can involve a loss of conscious thought. In other words, Spirit can 'move us to one side' and bring themselves completely into our bodies, using us to transmit their messages without us being aware of what they say or do. Be warned that this is only for very experienced mediums, who will have organised others to assist them during a demonstration for safety.

Our spirit guides are there to guide and inspire us and there is always one who is the doorkeeper guide, the 'bouncer' as it were, who makes sure that we remain safe. This guide will be with us from the moment we are born until we return to the spirit world, whilst other guides and helpers will come along as and when we need them. As I always say, we do not get a university professor-type if we are at the beginning of our journey, the primary school level; but when we are ready to go forward to the next stage another guide will appear.

On this particular evening at college, my assessor explained the procedure and told me that he would be with me for approximately half an hour, just to see that I was implementing the proper sort of teaching. I emphasised that if he were to leave then it must be before the meditation, because I didn't want to disturb the students who were going into a trance state. However, I needn't have worried. The assessor stayed until the end; he became fascinated with what was going on and, indeed, even went into meditation with the rest of the class.

At these times, I am often asked, "I don't seem to be able to connect with my guide, so what can I do?" The answer to this is that we must simply ask the spirit world to bring our guide to us, either by telling us or showing us. The answer will come. We need to be patient and remember that there is no time limit, trust in the energy of Spirit and it will be there when the time is right. We all have to start somewhere and if we are chosen to do this work then Spirit will help us on our journey.

Meditation is the best way for us to connect so try to do this at least three times a week. I still meditate now. Sometimes, with our busy lives, we have to make a real effort to do this, but it is worth it to get our connection and to have that calm time for ourselves.

My meditations still gave me messages from the spirit world and now I had much more contact with Abraham. He came with some profound knowledge, not just for me but for the whole world. For example, he told me that the world would unite when a catastrophe happened that would shake the world's leaders: this was the tsunami in Thailand when thousands of people were lost or missing, there was a worldwide outpouring of grief and leaders began to communicate with one another. Love and healing was sent from all those who were able to give healing.

People ask me why we are given knowledge – such as of this disaster – that we cannot do anything about, and indeed why we can't change the outcome. It is because we cannot change what is meant to happen, even if the tragedy is such that many lives are lost because of it. Sometimes we are given these things just to prove that the information we receive is the truth and we need to accept it as such. What we are experiencing in the world today has an impact on us all, and at times it seems that the dark is smothering the light; then the lightworkers, people who have love and light within their hearts, must act to outweigh 'the dark workers'. Sometimes these disasters, however they come, can unite all the lightworkers into making changes for the future.

BEING PREPARED

T here were a lot of changes at the college. A new Principal had taken over and there were rumours that part-time courses would be culled unless they were 'educationally beneficial'. Around this time, someone approached me to do some workshops for them in Wolverhampton, which I thought might be too much for me with my college and church work. But since the long summer holidays were coming I decided to do some short courses for them. Crowfoot had told me that 'the wind of change' was coming and to be prepared for it so I just went with the flow of things and knew that everything would work out eventually. Sadly, the college did decide not to renew my course, but the work in Wolverhampton took over – synchronicity and spirit knowledge once again coming good.

During meditation one morning, my Mum came to me and told me that she was preparing the way and I must tell the girls, meaning my sisters, that things would be okay. I was so worried about this that

81

I rang my Dad, who was quite upbeat and had a word with both my sisters just to make sure all was well. Again, I wrote everything down in my notebook and wondered what this was all about. Then a couple of days later, Mum came to me again in a dream. In this, we were living in the old house we had prior to our move to another area of Birmingham, and I was coming home from work and walking towards the house. Mum was standing by the gate.

"I'm here now, Mum, shall I put the kettle on?" I said.

"I'm not waiting for you," she replied, and stayed waiting at the gate.

When I awoke, I thought this very strange. But two days later I had a call from my cousin to say that my Auntie Jean was very ill and wasn't expected to last the night. Mum and Jean had been very near in age and were good friends as well as relatives, so Mum would have wanted to make sure she was alright when she passed.

We all receive information in dreams, when we are in an altered state of consciousness and Spirit can join us without giving us a scare. With my experiences, I am not afraid of seeing Spirit 'in person' but a lot of people would be. So a gentle way of communicating with us is through dream-like visions. We know it's different when we have one of these dreams because they are very vivid and we remember them distinctly when we awake. It is almost as if they are in technicolour as well and they stand out in the mind; someone once told me it was like being in the cinema and seeing everything enlarged on the screen, which is a good analogy. So it's a good idea always to take our little notebook to bed with us so that we can jot down the memories of these visions, because somewhere along the way the message will become clear and the vision will make sense.

A gentleman came to me for a reading and afterwards we began talking. He was on the committee of a small theatre and asked whether I would be interested in doing a fundraising event for them. I was taken aback but agreed to do it. The theatre only held ninety people and was in a residential area with hardly any car parking space, so the funds raised would provide the means to create a car park on the derelict ground behind the theatre that they had just purchased. It was all arranged and I was surprised to see the theatre full of people when I arrived.

While I was in the dressing room area of the theatre, a gentleman from the spirit world came through and was very cross with me for being there! He told me that I had no right to be in this theatre, there were standards to be met and moreover he didn't know who had allowed this to happen. I told him that I was there to improve the place so that more people could attend; the new car park would also stop the local residents complaining and getting up petitions to close the theatre. He seemed satisfied by this and faded away. Talking to the committee members and describing this man to them later, it became evident that this man was the old theatre manager who had been very stuck in his old-fashioned ways. He had gone to the spirit world over two years before and they were surprised by his message, but they all smiled at his manner because this was his character when he had been living.

When this man had gone, Crowfoot appeared and said that there was a man wanting to speak to 'Margaret', who would be in the audience. Crowfoot told me he would bring him forward when I started to work. I trusted this so, although I was very nervous about being in a theatre and doing clairvoyance, I knew Spirit wouldn't let me down.

The moment I stood on the stage, I felt the energy surge through me. I told the audience that I needed to speak to Margaret and immediately a hand went up. Thankfully there was only one Margaret in the audience but in any case, when a message is being given, the medium knows whether they have the right link or not and it does get sorted out. The man from the spirit world stepped in; he wanted to give her a bunch of daffodils as it was her birthday and he always gave her these, he said. Margaret nodded and I relayed more of the message.

"You were not supposed to be here tonight," I said. "This was all last minute but Spirit knew you would be here because your husband, Tom, wanted you to know that he is alright and back to his normal self. He was in a coma before he passed and didn't get a chance to say goodbye." There was a gasp from Margaret as well as from her daughter sitting next to her. Other bits of information were given and Margaret was in tears by the end. It transpired that her husband had had cancer and died only very recently, but she had sent her thoughts out to him and asked him to let her know he was out of pain. Margaret had not planned to be here this evening; her daughter had bought tickets for herself and a friend, but at the last minute her friend had to cancel because her son was ill so Margaret had stepped in to accompany her daughter.

So you see, I have faith in what Spirit tells me and know it will be correct although it might be unexpected at the time. Things work out in the right way, at the right time and for the right reason. I also feel gratitude to Spirit for helping me and for their protection, never taking my gift for granted and trying to work for the higher good. I am very aware of the vulnerability of people who are grieving and I treat them with the respect and responsibility that is needed on these occasions. Yes, the theatre raised enough money to start making the car park.

Soon after this, I decided to visit a fellow medium called Sue with whom I'd become friendly. (We had started a 'quest' together which was becoming ever more fascinating, a story that will be told at another time.) She said that she had received a message from my Uncle Sid that Bill, my Dad, was ill and that things would change towards the end of the year for him and for me, so I must be prepared. Dad and I were in contact on a regular basis although I hadn't been given any indication that he was ill at this time; still, as the message had come from Spirit I knew that they were preparing me for the outcome.

It would take a lot of persuasion to get Dad to see a doctor so it was quite a surprise when he asked my sister, who works in a doctor's surgery, to make an appointment for him. He had been suffering with pain in his back and his stomach for some time and it was getting worse. This was in August. He was sent for several tests and scans, which found that he had cancer everywhere; he was admitted to hospital and died in October.

To see a strapping man shrink before my eyes was devastating. One day when I visited him, he opened his eyes and looked at me saying, "What are doing here again, Bett?" This was my mother's name so I knew she had been to see him and was waiting for him. I do look very much like my Mum, so maybe Dad mistook me for her – or had he, since his eyes were only open for a short time? I held his hand and prayed he would go over to Spirit very soon.

My sister had booked a holiday in Mexico for this September; we had discussed it all and I'd said that nothing would happen in the couple of weeks of her being away. It was a once-in-a-lifetime holiday and they had booked it eighteen months earlier. I'd made a note of all the appropriate telephone numbers and promised her faithfully that if anything should happen we would contact her immediately so she could come home. In the two weeks she was gone, Dad deteriorated so much that he was hardly recognisable when my sister returned. She was the organised one of us and if anything needed to be done we would always call on her and know that she would get it arranged. Dad knew this too and I'm sure he was waiting to see her, even though he didn't seem to be in the conscious world at all. My sister arrived straight from the `plane to see him and told him he could go now because she was here and would sort everything out. Within the next two hours he had died, knowing that everything was in safe hands.

My father's death was a shock to me and the clearing of his house was quite a task for the three of us siblings. It was also poignant as there were many things we came across that Dad had kept, including old photographs of family we had not been in touch with for a long time. Everyone grieves differently, there is no right or wrong way of doing it, and it was six months later when I realised fully that my Dad was no longer here to talk to and ask advice of. Something had happened in the family and I automatically picked up the telephone to tell him the news. Consciously I knew he was gone, but in that moment it hit me again. I'm sure that many people can relate to this. I now know that Dad is guiding me and my sisters from the spirit world.

Time was passing quickly now and my work for Spirit meant I was extremely busy with churches, workshops and other spiritual events taking place. My family was growing, I had become a great-grand-mother and family gatherings were part and parcel of my life too. Life was a lot more settled now, I loved my work and was always guided by the spirit world in whatever I did. Crowfoot had been telling me for a while that 'words must be written to inspire people' and all that had happened to me should be put into a book. I'd thought about this but time always seemed to run away from me. Now he told me again to write a book about my spiritual journey, and that he would give me a sign to let me know when the time was right…

Spirit is willing but the body is frail

Time flew by and, at the next New Year, I began to wonder what changes would be happening. Crowfoot told me once again to 'be prepared' because a new chapter was about to begin, my work as it was would change and may even have to come to a stop for a while. I was quite perturbed by this but realised that I must just get on with what was being given: what is meant to be will be.

And not long into this year came a health scare for my husband, Don. He worked at a recycling centre and sometimes, when it is closed, rubbish bags are dumped at the entrance. It was while picking up one of these bags that a used needle jabbed his leg and led to blood poisoning. He was ill with this for some time and then the investigations and blood tests that followed revealed that he had diabetes. Don was not someone who went to the doctor for anything and, indeed, he very rarely had days off work (four days in the twenty years I had known him), so he was very impatient when this happened. Although his recovery was slow, I realised that this was meant to be because, if the injury had not happened, we would not have discovered that he was suffering with diabetes and that would have had even more diabolical consequences for him.

My workshops in Wolverhampton came to an end but, as one door closes, another door opens. I was at Bromsgrove Spiritualist Church giving a service when one of the committee members approached me and asked whether I could run some development workshops for them. Of course, I wouldn't decline because Bromsgrove was where I began my development and I have an affection for the church. I wanted to help as well, because this knowledge needs to be put out there so that people may gain an understanding of what the Spiritualist churches can offer and of what the connection with Spirit is all about. There is a thirst for knowledge and I wanted to help others learn to become workers for the spirit world. So another new chapter started.

I was having a few glitches with my own health as well, such as swelling in my legs which, after several visits to the doctor, was diagnosed as cellulitis. But I had committed myself to my eighteen-week syllabus at the church and I was determined to be well enough for that. Harborne Spiritualist Church approached me to do some of my workshops there too, so the teaching was more at the forefront of my work for Spirit. I was happy about this, although when you are booked as a medium your diary begins to get full, sometimes two years in advance. Fitting all this in with serving churches at the same time meant I was very busy and it was testing my energy levels to the limit. I asked Spirit to send me the help I needed because I knew I couldn't keep up this pace without it.

There were many people joining up to the development classes in Bromsgrove and among these was a lady called Joan. Around the fourth week of the course and near the end of the class, I was so weary with my legs hurting badly; all I really wanted to do was get home, have a cup of tea with my feet up and have a rest. Joan approached me and said that she had just retired from work and therefore had more spare time now, so I just needed to ask if there was anything she could do to help me. I thanked her for the offer but, as usual, dismissed it because of my independent streak – I could manage. However, Crowfoot had told me that whilst they wanted me to continue the work, they were preparing for me to be 'resting soon' and would be sending help.

A few weeks later, seeing that I was still struggling, Joan again asked if she could help by at least being my driver when I attended churches to do clairvoyant evenings. Again, I thanked her and went home not thinking too much about the offer. But next day, during a meditation, Crowfoot was angry! He said, "I have sent the help and it is up to you to accept it."

By now, I really was very weary, it was becoming harder to keep everything going and I was struggling. So the following week I had a conversation with Joan about her driving for me and we decided to meet up and have a meal to discuss whether it was feasible for us to work something out. I was being cautious because, as a medium serving churches and giving workshops in different places, I needed someone who wouldn't impact on my energy so that I could to do my work. Well, we soon hit it off; in fact, the first meeting lasted at least four hours while we talked and talked, and this was the beginning of a wonderful friendship that we still enjoy today.

Joan took over the driving for me, which enabled me to carry on with the work for Spirit. I love the work and I am always humbled by the responses I get when the messages are imparted. Joan and I would often have a giggle on the way to a church, which would lift my energy. I would sometimes be receiving some information during these times, or even the night before, about what I needed to say to someone in the church. I never know the people who attend the churches and I prefer that, because then you know it is coming from Spirit and not from my own subconscious.

One time, when serving a church, a young man who had committed suicide came through and wanted to give information to his Mum, but she wasn't at the church; however, a neighbour who was also a friend had come along. She was able to understand all the information. But one poignant part of the message was for this lady herself, when he reminded her that she had helped him when he was younger by giving him a bed for the night, with his Mum's approval, because of problems he was having. Sometimes it happens this way, and as long as the message gets to the right person then the spirit world is happy.

The development group were enjoying their journey and part of the learning was a session with table-tilting. This phenomenon needs to be done in controlled situations with someone experienced in attendance. When we do it in the development class, I 'clear' the tables and put a protection around them. What do I mean by this? This means burning sage and surrounding the tables with it, which clears any residual energy that the tables are holding so there won't be any disturbing energy for newcomers using the tables. I then put my hands on the tables and ask my guides to surround them with their energy of love and light and protection.

The students sit in small groups around a table with their hands lightly on the top, sometimes only their fingertips. Playing loud music also gets the energy going. Then they watch in amazement as the table tilts to the left and right, and sometimes they have to get out of their chairs to follow the table as it dances around the room! It is great fun and the messages received are very good for the students as well. However, it is certainly not a parlour game and should only be demonstrated for the purpose of teaching. It shows how Spirit can make things happen even in a physical way.

Table-tilting is one example of 'physical phenomena' and another is when Spirit send 'apports', items materialising from the spirit world onto the Earth plane. There are many apports in the Arthur Findlay museum, one of which is an actual postcard from someone in the spirit world. This came during a trance session with a well-known medium at the college. Whilst giving a message to a girl from Germany, the medium asked her to open the palm of her hand to receive a message from her sister; as the medium put her hand above the girl's, the post-card appeared.

I look at my students when I tell them the story and ask, "Do you know what it said?" They are always agog, mesmerised by it all. Then I smile and say, "Wish you were here!" and much laughter ensues. A sense of humour is something that has kept me going throughout my challenging life, and when I serve churches and give workshops I always try to bring a bit of humour into the work. People remember things more if there are smiles and laughter during the teaching, whilst laughter lifts the energy during services too, enhancing it so that the links with Spirit become stronger.

Around this time, Don and I came to realise that the advice we'd been given to take out an interest-only mortgage was now becoming a liability to us. Such schemes were common at that time, intended to clear the mortgage when one retires; but poor interest rates meant that this was no longer possible for us. On top of that, Don was made redundant twelve months before he was due to retire, all of which meant that we would have to sell our lovely bungalow. I was extremely upset by this but knew it was what we would have to do to keep us financially solvent. However, this was also just at the time of a slump in the market and the bungalow was up for sale for quite a time. We had until the following April to sell it before we would go under, so this was an extremely stressful period for us both, with Christmas approaching.

The end of the development group in Bromsgrove was also nigh. We'd had some lovely times together and I said I would do all I could to try and continue the development of the few who wanted to go further. I had made some lovely friends and it had been a brilliant class with much potential; I do know that many of them have gone on to pursue their own spiritual pathway.

Crowfoot assured me that everything would be alright but to be prepared to stop for a while. This message was now on repeat every time I connected with him. Indeed, one time when Abraham came he brought me the healing presence of Archangel Michael, who 'gave' me a sword to be the warrior fighting through all challenges. My notebook was filled with these last messages. I was very weary but my stubbornness and my determination not to let people or Spirit down kept me going.

The New Year dawned, we had still not sold the bungalow so I sat down in despair and asked my Dad to come and help if he could. Then out of the blue we started to have appointments made to view the property. Two were booked on one particular day, one in the morning and the other in the afternoon. My Dad had worked for Mitchells and Butlers brewery from the moment he left school until he retired; when the first people arrived to view the bungalow, the gentleman spoke of having worked as a delivery driver for M & B for many years. My goodness, I thought, this truly was a sign. The one in the afternoon was even more bizarre as they happened to have the same surname as my maiden name. This couple were very keen and put in an offer, which we accepted. I knew my Dad had indeed been helping me.

Now it was all systems go, packing and making sure that everything was in order. We could not afford to buy again because there was not enough equity in the bungalow, so we had to look for somewhere suitable to rent. I also had to cancel some venues due to the stress of all this. To tell the truth, I knew that this is what we had to do but my heart was breaking as well because we'd had a happy few years in that bungalow.

My eldest daughter, Michelle, came with us to view a few rental properties but they were all unsuitable and we were now getting to the point when we needed to find something soon. All the family were on the lookout for us; my youngest daughter had sent over an Internet link to a bungalow she had found, but we thought it too far away at the time. Then one rainy day, when we had viewed two promising properties but were very despondent because neither turned out to be suitable, we sat in Michelle's house having a cuppa. She was scouring the Internet on our behalf and came across the same one my youngest daughter had mentioned. Suddenly she stood up.

"I've just been told we need to see it," she said. We looked at her, left our tea on the table and went off to see where this bungalow was. When we arrived, we liked the area after all and were just taking down the details from the 'To Let' board when someone drew up in a car, followed by a lady from the estate agency. Being cheeky, we asked if we could have a quick look around while she was there, explaining that we were looking for a long-term rental. The other couple, young with children, had a look at it first but told the estate agent that they didn't feel it was suitable for them.

It was for us! But if we hadn't gone when we did, we would have missed the opportunity to view it and Spirit had inspired my daughter to get us to move fast. It was a lovely bungalow and, although it was further out than we really wanted to be, it suited our needs. So we moved and began to feel settled.

In this small village there was a GP practice with the old-fashioned sort of doctors who got to know their patients and took the time to understand them better. My doctor was sorting out my medications and seemed concerned about the continued swelling in my legs and feet. I told her that I really hadn't got time to be ill; she smiled and just said that she wanted to keep an eye on me. These doctors were also sorting out Don's medication for his diabetes, as it seems he was on the wrong tablets and injections for him. I'm sure we needed to go to this small village, to get our health back on track.

Joan and I were still driving to the various venues and I had promised the development group that I would get some of them working from the rostrum in the church. One night I arranged this for a small group of them, and they all did it. But I wanted to show them more about how it works so I got up and promptly gave everyone a message, showing the students as I went along how I was doing it. This is not my normal practice: when you're teaching it is about the students, not the teacher. But somehow, I don't know why, I thought that I may not see them again for some time… Even though we arranged for another night like this, it turned out just as Crowfoot had suggested and I had to stop for a while.

Within a week, I had to go to the doctor's surgery for a blood pressure check. On the same day, a friend was coming to see me but I thought the process wouldn't take long and I would soon be back home to see her. I arrived at the designated time, the doctor took my blood pressure and then examined my heart. It appeared that I was about to have a heart attack and was rushed into hospital! This completely knocked me off my feet. Luckily, my condition was stabilised in hospital and I was allowed home later in the evening. However, the hospital doctor warned me that I'd had a lucky escape and, if I didn't slow down and have complete rest, I might not be so fortunate in the future.

All my bookings and workshops had to be cancelled and, bless her, Joan took over and helped to smooth the way. Still, the process of handing my business mobile 'phone over to her was devastating. I thought that all my work of many years was coming to an end and I didn't want it to stop. My very reason for being, my self-worth, was in serving Spirit and giving knowledge where I could, so how was I going to be able do that if everything was coming to an end? I went into panic mode, my thoughts all over the place, and I was really cross with Spirit and with Crowfoot for 'allowing' this to happen to me.

Although Joan was cancelling venues and churches, in my own mind this was just a blip – I would recover and return to what I had been doing before. But Spirit had other ideas. I was just recovering from the heart scare when I caught a bad case of shingles, then the MS became a little worse and I also began to suffer with cataracts in both eyes. Crowfoot had been right all along, I did have to stop for a while and relinquish the thought of returning to work in the way I had been doing for many years.

But, of course, my work for Spirit was not over. Whilst I was doing much less in the churches and only the odd workshop at certain venues, I realised that my work needed to go in a different direction, one that wouldn't have such an impact on my energy levels. This was when I formed the eighteen-week spiritual development syllabus into six workbooks. These are now being made into one book, to support all fledgling mediums and others who have a curiosity about spiritual development. I also investigated how I could get people to understand their own energies by creating an online course about the gut instinct: it's called 'Empower the Hidden You' and is on Udemy.com.

So my spiritual work is not over, it has just changed direction.

THE PURPOSE OF IT ALL

My life has had many twists and turns, but throughout it all I have believed that someone walks with me and helps me along the way. I was born to serve in the way I have, so my spiritual purpose began when I first drew breath. An astrologer who drew up my chart many years ago told me that from an early age I already had spiritual knowledge – it was all there in the stars.

It's true, throughout the many pathways that life has presented to me, I have always known that I could see, hear and sense Spirit around me. These gifts are called clairvoyance (seeing), clairaudience (hearing) and clairsentience (sensing). It was only later, when I began touring the Midlands serving the churches, that my knowledge grew and I realised that this was what I was born to do all along.

My many challenges have given me insights
into how to deal with adversity.

They have given me empathy and an understanding of life's difficulties for others. As you will have read, there is not a lot I haven't experienced and this has given me an even greater reason to keep going on my journey, to help those in need. My spiritual light still has a beam that encompasses others as well as myself. However, I am not a Wonder Woman who can sort everything out and have never claimed to be: I am just an ordinary woman blessed with an extraordinary gift, and I am humbled by it.

I believe that when we decide to come back to the Earth we have an inkling about what it is that we want to achieve. This time around, I feel that my choice was to enlighten and to help as many people as I could, either with one-to-one readings or from the rostrum. Maybe it was also to enrich others' journeys by learning all about the spiritual aspects of life, through my teaching work. Many people wonder about fate, whether we have control over everything we do or whether our lives are being mapped out for us. It's a question that has many answers. But remember, we do choose this life plan and what we want to achieve. Along the way, help is given to us even though often we do not realise it is there.

I think that life's pathway is rather like going from Birmingham to London on the M1! Along the way there are many hold-ups, and along part of the way the motorway may be closed, causing us to divert. Yet on those diversions we meet other people and travel down different roads with them, experiencing many things; these may be good or bad or unexpected but they all influence the progress of our journey. Ultimately, everyone's destination is to go back to the spirit world via as many roads as our paths take us – but it's not about the destination, what's important is what we learn on the journey.

This is the analogy I have lived by, although of course I cannot pretend it has been easy. Yet the spiritual happenings along the way have always proved to me that when we believe and we ask for guidance, we are shown the way. This may not be exactly the way we thought or hoped that things might happen, but when we look back later on events we realise that if they hadn't happened then we would not have done or achieved what we did. To my mind, coincidence doesn't happen – what is meant to be will be. The pathway is set and we must travel along it, learning about and understanding our own spirituality within us. Everyone can access this truth. Religious belief may be a comfort for some whilst for others it can be difficult. I like to remember this saying by Peg Huxtable, which speaks to us all:

"When life seems difficult and the road ahead is steep, remember that God didn't make the Earth flat, and it is more interesting and beautiful because of that."

Spirituality is the key and learning to love life, ourselves and others, is a commitment we must all make because the human race has so much to learn to live in peace with one another. As individuals, our learning should never stop.

When I return to my destination in the spirit world, I want my purpose this time round to have been achieved. I want my legacy to be that people will remember me not by my name but for the learning they have received, the messages from Spirit during my rostrum work or the one-to-one message that has been profound and made a difference to them. I am only the instrument passing these things on and hope that I do this with love and caring.

When you are trying to understand your own purpose in life, think about what it is that you intend to achieve. How determined are you? Does the pathway you are on give you fulfilment and happiness in your life? And if you find yourself still 'wanting', why haven't you made changes? When we stop to think about it all, we can see that the best solution to the problem of understanding our purpose is to turn our challenges into opportunities to change our lives. Do not be afraid! We all have a guardian angel and a spirit guide to help us and they will show us the way when we call on them.

One day, Joan and I decided to go out for the day. There was no thought about where we were going, although prior to this I had asked

Spirit for a bit of direction from them for the next phase of my spiritual life. So we packed a picnic, got in the car and just started to drive towards Worcestershire. On the way, Joan suddenly spotted a signpost to a church off the main road and her car just seemed to move in that direction of its own accord. There had been no intention for this to happen and indeed, when we got to the church, Joan said, "I don't think we need to go into the church but into the graveyard."

Before I relate the story, I need to remind you that my natural father's full name was Joseph Henry Nash and that my birth name was Pamela Ann Nash. Moreover, Crowfoot had told me several times that I need to tell the story of my personal life as well as describing all the spiritual events along the way. He told me that I was to inspire others by showing that, even in adversity, having faith will help us through the most desperate of times.

Joan was drawn to a particular place so into the graveyard we went, to the gravestone she had identified that had an angel carved on the top. The name on the stone was Ann Nash and this lady's son, also buried in the grave, was called Henry Joseph Nash. We had been quite randomly and unexpectedly directed towards this church and I took this as a sign from Crowfoot that the writing of my story needed to be done from the very beginning of my life's journey.

This was the answer to my question, my request for direction. Spirit had spoken. It was time to write this book!

My work for Spirit will only stop when my last breath is taken, which hopefully will not be for a long time yet. Crowfoot assures me that I still have a great deal of work to do, so I will continue willingly and try to educate as many people as I can along the way about spirituality.

Well, no-one can predict what will happen tomorrow. I just know that during my years of working with Spirit they have always guided me towards the paths I needed to be on. My guides and helpers have been with me every step of the way. The book of my life has had many different chapters and each chapter has given me a sense of my own purpose in this lifetime.

Now, everyone can use their spiritual abilities, we are all born to be spiritual, and even the sceptics I have come across have understood that there is more to Heaven and Earth than we can ever know. Learning to meditate and to listen for the wisdom of our guides will help us understand that connection. Everyone has their own gifts, so go forward and remember that for you, as for me, Spirit shows the way!

IF YOU HAVE ENJOYED THIS BOOK...

Local Legend is committed to publishing the very best spiritual writing, both fiction and non-fiction. You might also enjoy:

DAY TRIPS TO HEAVEN

T J Hobbs (ISBN 978-1-907203-99-2)

The author's debut novel is a brilliant description of life in the spiritual worlds and of the guidance available to all of us on Earth as we struggle to be the best we can. Ethan is learning to be a guide but having a hard time of it, with too many questions and too much self-doubt. But he has potential, so is given a special dispensation to bring a few deserving souls for a preview of the afterlife, to help them with crucial decisions they have to make in their lives. The book is full of gentle humour, compassion and spiritual knowledge, and it asks important questions of us all.

A UNIVERSAL GUIDE TO HAPPINESS

Joanne Gregory (ISBN 978-1-910027-06-6)

Joanne is an internationally acclaimed clairaudient medium with a celebrity contact list. Growing up, she ignored her evident psychic abilities, fearful of standing out from others, and even later, despite witnessing miracles daily, her life was difficult. But then she began to learn the difference between the psychic and the spiritual, and her life turned round. This is her spiritual reference handbook – a guide to living happily and successfully in harmony with the energy that created our universe. It is the knowledge and wisdom distilled from a lifetime's experience of working with Spirit.

THE QUIRKY MEDIUM

Alison Wynne-Ryder (ISBN 978-1-907203-47-3)

Alison is the co-host of the TV show *Rescue Mediums*, in which she puts herself in real danger to free homes of lost and often malicious spirits. Yet she is a most reluctant medium, afraid of ghosts! This is her amazing and often very funny autobiography, taking us 'back stage' of the television production as well as describing how she came to discover the psychic gifts that have brought her an international following.

This book won the Silver Medal in the national Wishing Shelf Book Awards.

SIMPLY SPIRITUAL

Jacqui Rogers (ISBN 978-1-907203-75-6)

The 'spookies' started contacting Jacqui when she was a child and never gave up until, at last, she developed her psychic talents and became the successful international medium she is now. This is a powerful and moving account of her difficult life and her triumph over adversity, with many great stories of her spiritual readings. The book was a Finalist in The People's Book Prize national awards.

AURA CHILD

A I Kaymen (ISBN 978-1-907203-71-8)

One of the most astonishing books ever written, telling the true story of a genuine Indigo child. Genevieve grew up in a normal London family but from an early age realised that she had very special spiritual and psychic gifts. She saw the energy fields around living things, read people's thoughts and even found herself slipping through time, able to converse with the spirits of those who had lived in her neighbourhood. This is an uplifting and inspiring book for what it tells us about the nature of our minds.

5P1R1T R3V3L4T10N5

Nigel Peace (ISBN 978-1-907203-14-5)

With descriptions of more than a hundred proven prophetic dreams and many more everyday synchronicities, the author shows us that, without doubt, we can know the future and that everyone can receive genuine spiritual guidance for our lives' challenges. World-renowned biologist Dr Rupert Sheldrake has endorsed this book as "...vivid and fascinating... pioneering research..." and it was national runner-up in The People's Book Prize awards.

CELESTIAL AMBULANCE

Ann Matkins (ISBN 978-1-907203-45-9)

A brave and delightful comedy novel. Having died of cancer, Ben wakes up in the afterlife looking forward to a good rest, only to find that every-one is expected to get a job! He becomes the driver of an ambulance (with a mind of her own), rescuing the spirits of others who have died suddenly and delivering them safely home. This book is as thought-provoking as it is entertaining.

TAP ONCE FOR YES

Jacquie Parton (ISBN 978-1-907203-62-6)

This extraordinary story offers powerful evidence of human survival after death. When Jacquie's son Andrew suddenly committed suicide, she was devastated. But she was determined to find out whether his spirit lived on, and began to receive incredible yet undeniable messages from him... Several others also then described deliberate attempts at spirit contact. This is a story of astonishing love and courage, as Jacquie fought her own grief and others' doubts in order to prove to the world that her son still lives.

Further details and extracts of these
and many other beautiful books may be seen at
www.local-legend.co.uk